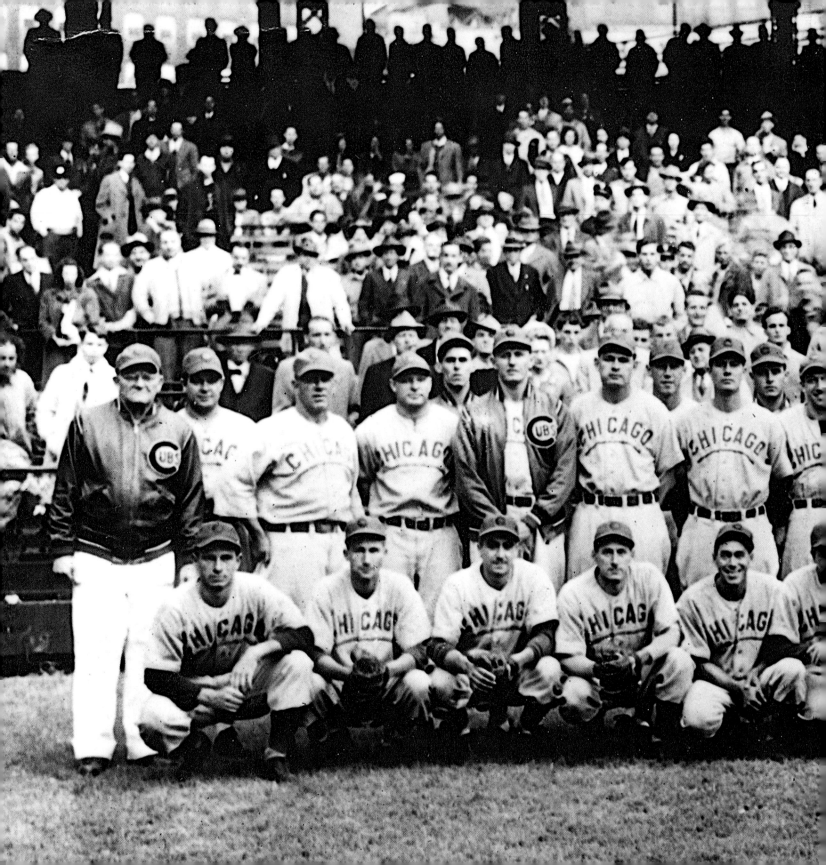

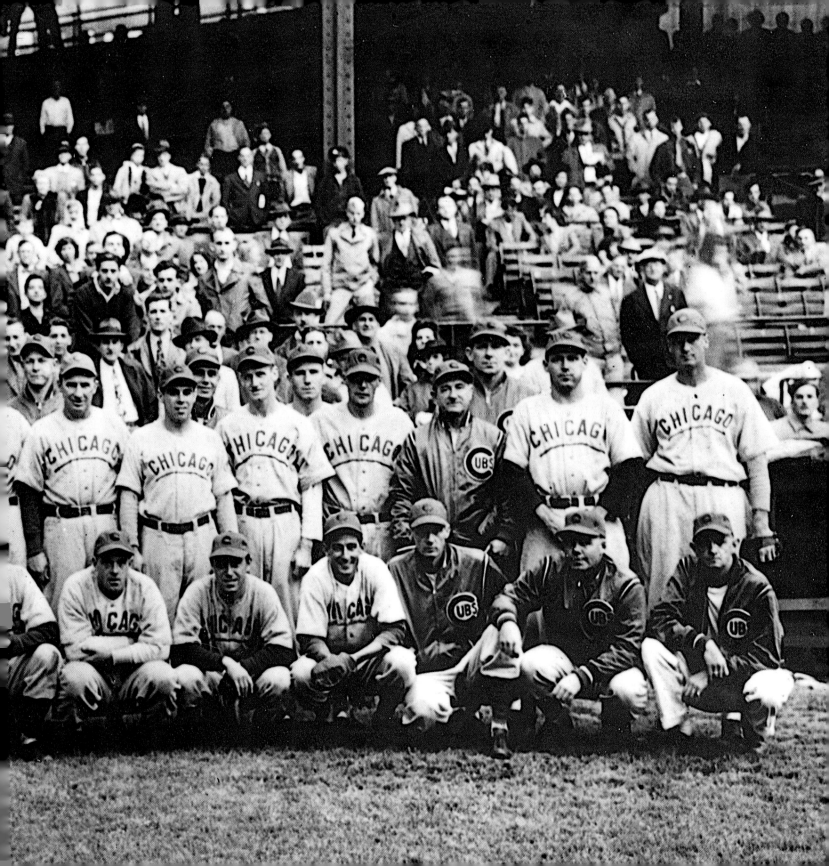

THE CHICAGO CUBS

MEMORIES AND
MEMORABILIA OF
THE WRIGLEY WONDERS

Text by Bruce Chadwick
Photography by David M. Spindel

ABBEVILLE PRESS · PUBLISHERS
New York · London · Paris

Pages 2-3: The 1945 National League champs (see p. 84). Frontispiece: This colorful collection covers just about every era in the Cubs' long and colorful history. Title page: A Cubs tobacco tin from around 1910. This page: A collection of tickets recalls many happy days at Wrigley Field. Table of Contents: A program from 1952 (see p. 92); legendary shortstop Joe Tinker (see p. 39); Pins commemorating Ryne Sanderg (see p. 122) and Ernie Banks (see p. 97); a memento from the pennant-winning 1932 season (see p. 73); and a ticket to the 1929 World

To Margie and Rory.
—B. C.

For a special friend, Max Lowenherz, who has always believed in me and supported my photography over the past thirty years.
—D. M. S.

EDITOR: Stephen Brewer
DESIGNERS: Virginia Pope & Patricia Fabricant
PRODUCTION EDITOR: Owen Dugan
PRODUCTION SUPERVISOR: Matthew Pimm

Library of Congress Cataloging-in-Publication Data
Chadwick, Bruce.
The Chicago Cubs : memories and memorabilia of the Wrigley wonders / text by Bruce Chadwick ; photography by David M. Spindel.
p. cm.
Includes bibliographical references (p.) and index.
ISBN 1-55859-513-9
1. Chicago Cubs (Baseball team)—History. 2. Chicago Cubs (Baseball team)—Collectibles. I. Title
GV875.C6C43 1994
796.357'64'0977311—dc20
93-21376
CIP

First edition.

ACKNOWLEDGMENTS

We would like to thank all the collectors and fans who talked to us about their collections and memorabilia and let us photograph them at stores, museums, homes, card shows, restaurants, and stadiums. We are particularly grateful to Bruce Gold and the Gold family of Skokie, Illinois, who let us spend an entire day with them, and Dan Knolls, who not only let us photograph his collection but even found us a warehouse to do it in. Thanks also to Joshua Evans, of Leland's, the New York sports auction house, for his assistance, and to the helpful researchers at the National Baseball Hall of Fame, at Cooperstown, particularly to its photo director, Patricia Kelly.

We'd also like to thank the Cubs' public relations director Sharon Pannozzo and her staff, as well as all the ushers at Wrigley Field who let us go where we weren't supposed to go. The athletes who talked to us were also helpful, particularly Ernie Banks, Ron Santo, Phil Cavarretta, and Billy Williams.

Finally, our special thanks to editors Stephen Brewer, Amy Hughes, Owen Dugan, Constance Herndon, and Phillip Reynolds and to Virginia Pope and Patricia Fabricant, our designers, who worked with us to make this another fine volume in the Major League Memories series.

—BRUCE CHADWICK AND DAVID SPINDEL

CONTENTS

OFFICIAL PROGRAM 10¢

CHICAGO CUBS · WRIGLEY FIELD

WORLD'S CHAMPIONS

RYNE SANDBERG

THE FRIENDLY CONFINES

It was 2:35 P.M. on a hot, sunny summer afternoon at Wrigley Field. The old ballpark was overflowing with people. All 38,710 seats were sold, some at forty dollars by scalpers, and thousands more fans were standing behind the field-level seats and behind the last row of the bleachers. The "bleacher bums" were in a glorious mood, chattering with each other, shouting encouragement over the thick, ivy-covered brick walls to the outfielders, who acknowledged them with smiles and waves of their gloves. Hundreds of men in the bleachers had their shirts off and their tans on, basking in the rays of the afternoon sun. Dozens of young women in cut-off jeans and bikini tops were doing the same. Beyond the walls of the ballpark, several thousand others partied and watched the game from the roofs of the ten apartment houses that overlook Wrigley. Thousands more, unable to get tickets, milled around the ballpark, listening to the game against the New York Mets on the radio as they sat on the curb or watched it on a television in Murphy's Bar and Grill on Sheffield Street or the Cubby Bear, on Addison. The Cubs' outdoor café was jammed with people. Souvenirs and T-shirts sold briskly at corner stands. Out in left field, the "14" flag, for Ernie Banks, and the "26" flag, for Billy Williams, fluttered in the light breeze.

First baseman Mark Grace snapped shut his glove on the ball for the

Take them up to the ball game. Thousands of fans jam the neighborhood rooftops, some with barbecues, bars, and their own small bleachers, to watch the Cubs. The food's great and the view of the game, surprisingly, is very good.

Much of Wrigley and the neighborhood can be seen in this shot.

These pennants were produced over three generations.

final out of the top of the seventh inning and the Cubs players trotted off the grass of the field and onto the wooden floor of the dugout. As if on cue from a maestro, everyone in the park and on the buildings beyond stood up. Seventh-inning stretch time. All turned to stare at the WGN-TV booth in the press box. As he has done for every seventh inning at Wrigley for twelve years, announcer Harry Caray, America's voice of baseball after twenty-five years with the Cards and eleven with the crosstown White Sox, stood up. He leaned over the open window of the press box, a big smile on his face, his thick black glasses set firmly on his nose, and motioned (one-two-three) with his hand.

Then he leaned into the mike, now hooked up to the park's public address system, and began to sing as some forty thousand joined in:

Take me out to the ball game,
Take me out with the crowd.
Buy me some peanuts and Cracker
  Jack,
I don't care if I never get back.
For it's root, root, root for the Cubbies,
If they don't win it's a shame,
For it's one . . . two . . . three
Strikes you're out
At the old ball game.

Harry and "Take Me out to the Ball Game" (I'll sing it every day until I die," says Caray) are a Chicago fixture, like the trains rumbling past Wrigley on the Howard El, the boats moored on Lake Michigan, and the downtown Loop. And grand old Wrigley Field, built in 1914 and the third-oldest ballpark in the United States, is as much a piece of America as of baseball. The tiny bandbox, shoehorned into the North Side of town between Addison, Clark, Waveland, and Sheffield streets, is to American baseball what St.

Charlie Grimm has plenty to smile about in this 1945 World Series program. His Cubs won the pennant, thanks mostly to newly acquired hurler Hank Borowy, who won eleven games in eleven weeks, and Phil Cavarretta, who led the league in batting.

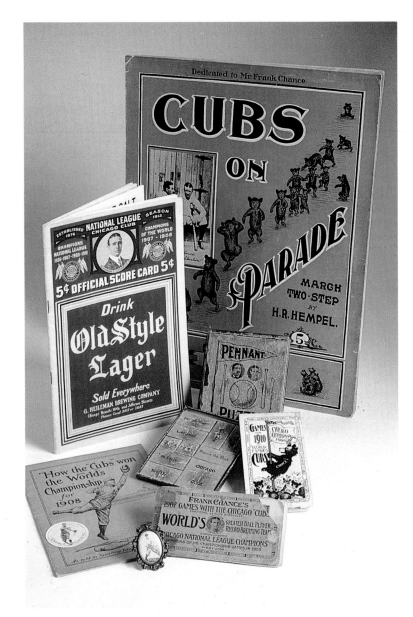

Everybody cele-
brated the Cubs in
Chicago from 1906
to 1920. H. R.
Hempel wrote a
song about them,
"Cubs on Parade,"
and the ballplayers'
faces seemed to
adorn every publica-
tion connected to
the team (Frank
Chance is on the
cover of the red
scorecard).

Peter's is to Rome and Notre Dame to
Paris; a wonderful old baseball cathedral,
built in a bygone era when the places
where people played and watched baseball
were not "stadiums" but "ballparks," and
the ballparks were built in crowded city
neighborhoods where the people were,
not distant suburbs where the highways
were. For most of this century, Wrigley,
like Fenway in Boston, has been the neighborhood's ballpark, and the Cubs have
been the neighborhood's team.

The neighborhood that surrounds
Addison and Clark is a middle-class blue-
collar, North Side neighborhood. There is
not much parking because most of the
fans just walk over. The streets are lined
with small apartment houses, two-family
homes, and 60-year-old single-family resi-
dences. It is an old urban neighborhood
like any other on the North Side, except
that it has this ballpark at its heart.

No team in baseball has the long and
rich tradition of the Cubs. Over the years
the team has won two world championships, ten pennants, and two divisional
titles. The Cubs have had 150 All-Star
Game selections and placed thirty-one
players in the Hall of Fame. Twenty-three
of their pitchers won twenty or more
games in a single year, and over 128 years
Cubs pitchers hurled ten no-hitters.

This Cubs National League schedule of 1941 was like those handed out by the league in many parks. It was about four by two inches, designed to be carried in a fan's pocket.

A fan somehow got his hands on this sign back in the 1930s and hung it in his basement.

The Cubs were not only charter members of the National League when it was founded in 1876, but were members of the old National Association of Professional Baseball Players when it started in 1871, just six years after the end of the Civil War. In those days, they were called the White Stockings and were often one of the best teams in baseball. The squad led by player-manager Cap Anson, King Kelly, and others even made baseball an international game by going on a first-ever, six-months' world tour in 1888–89. As the new century burst on the continent, the team, now called the Cubs, was to dominate the game, winning pennants in 1906, 1907, 1908, and 1910 and world championships in 1907 and 1908. They

were led by Hall of Fame pitcher Three-Finger Brown and the double-play team of Tinker, Evers, and Chance. With such talent, who could have guessed in 1908 that this would be the last World Series win?

But if Series wins didn't follow, many years of success within the National League did. The Cubs won pennants in 1918, 1929, 1932, 1935, 1938, and 1945, establishing themselves as one of baseball's great franchises. Along the way, the Cubs gave fans the chance to see some of the game's finest players, superstars like Grover Cleveland Alexander, Hank Borowy, Kiki Cuyler, Dizzy Dean, Gabby Hartnett, Billy Herman, Rogers Hornsby, Chuck Klein, and Hack Wilson.

Then, after losing the 1945 World Series, something happened. Baseball's express fell off the tracks. The Cubs never

The Cubs put out this special Hall of Fame certificate right after Banks was elected.

National Baseball
HALL OF FAME
August 8, 1977
Ernie Banks

The all-time home run king and all-time popularity champion of Chicago became known as "Mr. Cub" during a brilliant career that lasted from 1953 to 1971. He received, among his countless honors, the Most Valuable Player award for two straight seasons. He was named to the National League All-Star Team 13 times and hit a career total of 512 home runs.

PHOTOGRAPHY BY BARNEY STERLING

COPYRIGHT 1977 CHICAGO NATIONAL LEAGUE BALL CLUB (INC.)

won another pennant (they did win division titles in 1984 and 1989) and never won another World Series. Despite the continuing presence of great players in Cubs uniforms—people like Ernie Banks, Phil Cavarretta, Ron Cey, Mark Grace, Ken Holtzman, Fergie Jenkins, Don Kessinger, Greg Maddux, Ryne Sandberg, Ron Santo, Hank Sauer, Rick Sutcliffe, and Billy Williams—they have been wandering in the pennant desert longer than any other major league team. At least the equally distraught Red Sox, who haven't won a Series since 1918, made it to the October classic in 1967, 1975, and 1986, even if they lost all of them.

And yet, as the gloom deepened after 1945, the Chicago fans' love for the team grew. The more the Cubs struggled, the more fans cherished them and their marvelous old ballpark. Attendance has climbed steadily—from 635,000 in 1967 to 1.4 million in 1977 to 2.4 million in 1992. Thirty-six million more fans across the United States tune in to games on cable superstation WGN. And each win-

Tony Taylor, who spent just parts of three summers with the Cubbies, signed this ball for a fan in 1959.

ter, another 40,000 fans attend the annual Diehard Cubs Fans convention.

"The Cubs are part of your family. They are your city's team. You don't love them because they come in first. You love them because they play great baseball, and because your father loved them, and your grandfather loved them, and his grandfather loved them," said Dan Knolls, a lifelong Cubs fan and collector.

With no world championship in nine decades and no pennant since World War II, why do the Cubs generate such devotion? Why is ticket demand so high that you must wait on line in April just to buy bleacher seats? Why is Wrigley jammed to the rafters whenever the Cubs are home? This is one of baseball's great mysteries, whose answer is found not only in a long history of shared joy and suffering, but also somewhere in the loving way the crowd sings "Take Me out to the Ball Game." It's in the ivy, and the grass, and the rumble of the El going by, and, especially, it's in the kids playing ball in the streets beyond left field.

CHAPTER ONE

AROUND THE WORLD
1866 TO 1901

Chicago in 1866, at the close of the Civil War, was bursting at the seams. In just twenty-nine years, since it officially became a city, its population had exploded from 16,000 to more than 250,000. By the summer of 1866 it had become the major rail center of the United States, with lines going in and out of the city to every major American terminus plus Canada. The shipping industry, which used large clipper ships to crisscross Lake Michigan, was prosperous. Jobs and rails created a building boom that saw the entire southern side of Lake Michigan grow into a thriving, if congested, city. It was a city of immigrants. Newly arrived immigrants from southern and eastern Europe headed out of New York on the rails for Chicago. Scandinavians looking for farmland stopped there. From the south, the rails brought thousands of freed slaves.

They all needed jobs, shelter, and food, and they all needed entertainment. The entertainment had to be cheap, though, because this blue-collar city of rail workers and ship builders could not afford opera and ballet. It was the perfect setting for a game that people who knew nothing about sports or did not speak English could understand and play. The game was baseball.

Played on streets and in small neighborhood parks in Chicago in the

This ornate poster was produced during the National League's very first season. The Cubs, led by pitcher Albert Spalding (center) and slugger Ross Barnes (top) and Cap Anson (right center), won the pennant.

19

William Hulbert, president of the White Stockings (later the Cubs), founded the National League.

early 1850s, the game of baseball became wildly popular. During the Civil War, ballplayers brought their bats to battle and played baseball in army camps. Soldiers who didn't play it in Chicago before the war brought it back to their own neighborhoods when the conflict ended.

The game grew so rapidly in Chicago after the war that by 1866 there were sixty teams in the city and fifty more in surrounding towns in Illinois, more than in any other metropolitan area in America. These amateur "clubs" represented every social class, ethnic community, and profession, from law offices to lodges and factories. There were many all-black teams in the heavily segregated city, too.

In 1871, in an effort to establish teams that could attract large numbers of fans to parks for games, entrepreneurs organized the National Association of Professional Baseball Players of America, with the White Stockings (these were the original Cubs and no relation to the present-day Chicago White Sox) representing Chicago. The White Stockings helped take peoples' minds off the great Chicago fire of 1871, which destroyed seventeen thousand buildings and left a hundred thousand people homeless. The National Association was a worthy effort, but had too many teams and no fixed schedule. Gambling and fights in the stands were common. Stars from one team would suddenly jump to another to earn more money. By 1876, it was struggling.

Cap Anson was not only one of the game's finest players but also, as is clear from this Old Judge card, one of its snappiest dressers.

Few men have had as much impact on baseball as Albert Spalding. The Cubs first pitcher, he later became club president and took the team on its world tour in 1888–89. He also eliminated much of the gambling and disorderliness at most early ballparks and built a family market for the Cubs. In 1877 he started his wildly prosperous sporting goods business. Somewhere, somehow, someone in your family has had a piece of Spalding equipment over the years.

That same year, William Hulbert, the frustrated president of the White Stockings, urged the most successful and financially stable clubs to form the National League, a super organization that would capitalize on the thirst for baseball the NAPBP created but would avoid its mistakes. Chicago was a charter member, along with Cincinnati, St. Louis, Louisville, Hartford, New York, Boston, and Philadelphia. The new league gave fans an ironclad schedule of seventy games, ten against each opponent, affordable tickets (fifty cents), a national champion, and the best players in the land—all in large, clean ballparks.

A. G. SPALDING, PRESIDENT OF THE CHICAGO BASE BALL CLUB.

OLD JUDGE CIGARETTES   Goodwin & Co., New York.

The White Stockings had the best pitcher in the country, Al Spalding, on the mound. In that first season of play, at the Twenty-third Street Grounds, he would win forty-seven games for Chicago (Spalding went on to be president and part-owner of the Cubs and establish the Spalding sporting goods empire and all of its stores and catalogs). Ross Barnes led the league in batting that first year, with a withering .404 average. But the best of all was Adrian "Cap" Anson.

This is Cap Anson in one of his tougher looking poses. Anson was nicknamed "Cap" because in high school, college, and the pros he somehow always became captain of his team. He was the game's superstar from the first season, 1876, when he led the Cubs to a pennant with a .356 average, until his last, twenty-two years later, when he retired with a .329 average. As a manager, Anson won five pennants, was second four times, and had a record of 1,242 wins and 945 losses.

The tall, stocky Anson was no surprise. He had played professionally since 1871 in Rockford, Illinois, and Philadelphia before moving to the Chicago nine. He played third base during his first few years, but switched to first when he became player-manager in 1879. A dependable hitter, Anson led the league in batting three times, hit over .350 four times, and hit .343 that first season, quickly establishing himself as the game's first superstar. He would hit over .300 in twenty of his twenty-two seasons over his Hall of Fame career. He was as good a skipper as he was a player, managing the team to five pennants. He was a poor fielder, however, and still holds the all-time record for errors by a first baseman. (He was also a bigot and often refused to play teams with black players, helping to segregate baseball.)

With Anson, the White Stockings dominated the National League. They won the league's first game, 6-0, and went on to win pennants in 1876, 1880, 1881, 1882, 1885, and 1886. Some of the best players in early baseball played on those teams. John Clarkson came aboard in 1884 and the following year won fifty-three games. Mike "King" Kelly—who made base stealing such an exciting art form that a song, "Slide, Kelly, Slide," was

Old Judge cigarettes produced some of the first card sets. On the right is the magnificent King Kelly, whose sale to the Boston Braves for the unheard-of sum of ten-thousand dollars in 1887 was the talk of the town in Chicago for years. The card on the left pictures Ned Williamson, whose major league record of twenty-seven home runs, set in 1884, was not broken until Babe Ruth hit twenty-nine in 1919. He's with the team's feisty mascot, Willie Hahn.

23

Handsome Mike Kelly played for the Cubs from 1880 to 1886 and was one of the most popular players in all Chicago, hitting .354 in 1884 and .388 in 1886. His real skill was in stealing bases. He was electric. A song written about his base stealing ability, "Slide, Kelly, Slide," became the number-one sheet-music seller in the country.

written about him—played in the mid-1880s before being sold to Boston for ten thousand dollars, an astronomical sum in those days. Clark Griffith, who would later become owner of the Washington Senators, pitched in the 1890s.

The White Stockings not only topped the standings in most seasons but they revolutionized baseball in at least one important way. In 1885, they became the first team to hold spring training, practicing for a few weeks before the season in Hot Springs, Arkansas. They also, under Spalding's presidency, became pioneers of publicity, orchestrating such stunts as having Chicago catcher Pop Schriver grab a ball dropped from the top of the Washington Monument in 1893.

One of the finest strokes of publicity was the 1874 tour of Great Britain, when the team traveled abroad to show the British how baseball was played. In addition to several baseball games, the team played cricket matches against English teams. The 1874 jaunt went so well that later, in the winter of 1888–89, then team president Spalding and Anson took the Chicago nine and an "All American" professional club led by the New York Giants' John Montgomery Ward on an around-the-world tour. The tour and its publicity, abroad and at home, solidified

the White Stockings' position as America's most famous baseball team. It also brought the sport to three continents and the islands of the Pacific, with games in Hawaii, New Zealand, Australia, Egypt, continental Europe, and England—giving baseball an extraordinary amount of world exposure. The White Stockings' and All Americans' arrival in towns would be marked by parades after extensive publicity in local newspapers (Spalding was the master of hype). The towns always threw lavish dinners, lunches, and parties

This remarkable treasure is a rare photo of the **White Stockings** and the **All Americans**, the two teams that traveled around the world in an 1888–89 tour that put American baseball on the map. One game was played in a snowstorm in England and another at the foot of the pyramid of Cheops, in Egypt. Most surviving images of that team and tour are prints, not photos. A collector found this at a garage sale.

The American Baseball Team.

Their first appearance in England, Kennington Oval, March 12th, 1889

for the players, who met all the public officials and local dignitaries (including the Prince of Wales in England). In Hawaii they participated in a colorful luau with members of Hawaii's royal family. They played games on cricket pitches, race-tracks, college football fields, meadows—any kind of field that could be found. A December game in England was played on frozen turf after locals helped players shovel two inches of snow off it. And the most memorable game of all was played

The Cubs players who participated in the remarkable around the world tour in 1888–89 found the Sphinx as stonefaced as any National League umpire. The team, which toured with a congregation of league all-stars, played games in Hawaii, Australia, New Zealand, Egypt, Italy, France, and England, garnering much publicity for the game of baseball. They played one game in front of the pyramid of Cheops. Albert Spalding led the tour and tried to book the Roman Coliseum for a game (think of the concessions!) but the Italian government turned him down.

26

Around the World Tour
1888–1889

Chicago Club		All Americans	
ANSON	1b.	WARD	SS.
PFEFFER	2b.	CRANE	P.
WILLIAMSON	SS.	HEALY	F.
BURNS	3b.	FOGARTY	CF.
TENER	P.	WOOD	3b.
BALDWIN	P.	CARROLL	1b.
DALY	C.	BROWN	RF.
SULLIVAN	LF.	HANLON	LF.
RYAN	CF.	EARL	C.
PETTIT	RF.	MANNING	2b.

21

on a makeshift field set up at the foot of one of the pyramids in Egypt.

The team returned home to West Side Park, at Congress and Throop streets, for the 1889 season. (It was the club's third ballpark. The first was at Twenty-third Street. They spent two seasons there before playing at Lakefront Park, a wood-enclosed ballpark with a short, 180-foot-high left field fence right off Lake Michigan, from 1878 to 1884. They moved to West Side Park in 1885 and would be there through 1889. The White Stockings would later play at South Side Park, at Thirty-fifth and Wentworth

A lineup card from the first world baseball tour of 1888–89, the brainchild of Cap Anson and Albert Spalding, anchors this collage of Anson cards.

Clothiers and other stores handed out such coupons as this with impeccably dressed White Stockings on them to drum up business in the early 1880s.

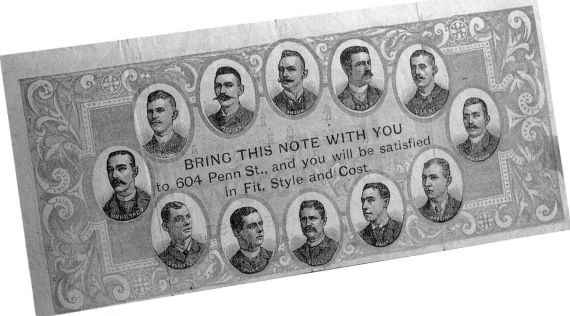

BRING THIS NOTE WITH YOU to 604 Penn St., and you will be satisfied in Fit, Style and Cost.

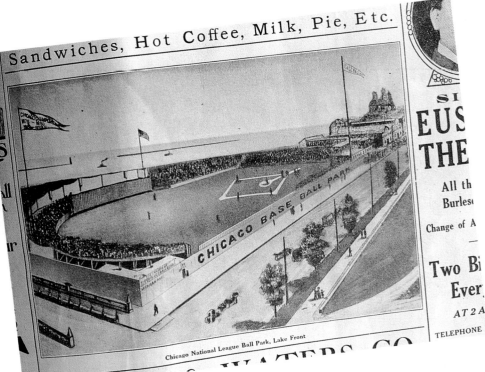

Sandwiches, Hot Coffee, Milk, Pie, Etc.

CHICAGO BASE BALL PARK

Chicago National League Ball Park, Lake Front

streets, from 1891 to 1894 and then their longtime home, West Side Grounds, at Polk and Wolcott streets, where they would be until 1916.)

There was now competition from several fronts. The rest of the National League started to catch up with the White Stockings. The team lost Kelly and Clarkson by 1890 and was diluted. The New York Giants came into the league in 1883, immediately drawing large crowds and attracting star players such as pitchers Tim Keefe and Smilin' Mickey Welch. In 1888 and 1889 they won pennants, besting Chicago. Brooklyn came into the National League in 1890 after winning the American Association flag in 1889 and won a pennant that first season.

This rare sketch from an 1880 news-paper shows Lakefront Park, the second home of the White Stockings. The team played at the park, built snugly against Lake Michigan at Michigan Avenue and Randolph Street, from 1878 to 1884 and won three pennants there.

Different teams had their own chewing tobacco tins in the 1880s. This was the Cubbies'.

The Goodwin Company issued hundreds of nicely drawn baseball cards in the 1880s.

Clockwise from top left: Jimmy Ryan, Tom Daly, Mike Sullivan, and two of Ned Williamson.

Chicago also had its hands full with upstart new leagues in the 1880s and lost ground to them, too. The Union Association, eyeing the success of the National, started play in 1884, but lasted only one season. The American Association, a well-financed and quite stable league, started in 1882, playing games on Sunday (which the conservative National League forbade), permitting the sale of beer at games (another NL no-no), and charging just a quarter for tickets. Although there was no team in Chicago, the league raised havoc with the National League by placing teams in some NL cities and even stealing away the Cincinnati Reds (owned by a brewery).

It was in 1890 that the greatest threat to the National League arrived in the form the Players' League. Hundreds of players, outraged by what they felt were unfair wages, left their National League teams and started their own organization with clubs in New York (two), Boston, Buffalo, Cleveland, Philadelphia, Pittsburgh, and the White Stockings' backyard, Chicago. All of them raided the National League and American Association clubs for players, taking away many of the stars and weakening their teams and gate appeal. During the summer of 1890 some of the National League clubs were on the

A finely drawn picture of **West Side Park** serves as the backdrop for this sketch of infielder Oliver "Patsy" Tebeau, which graces this 1899 program.

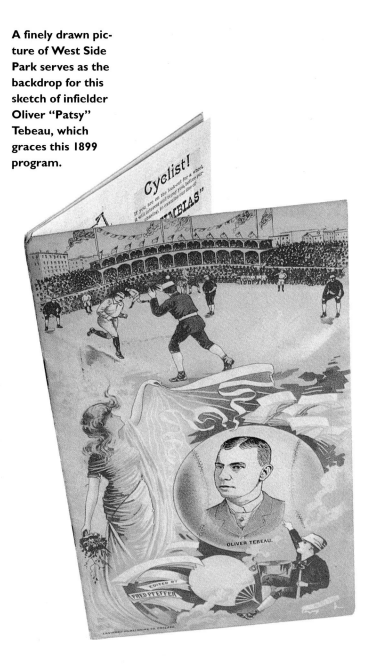

verge of bankruptcy because they lost attendance to the Players' League clubs. By 1890, Albert Spalding—who was not only the most influential man in baseball as president and part owner of the White Stockings but, because of his sporting goods empire, one of the richest men in America—led the counterattack on the Players' League. Spalding ordered his stores in Chicago to hand out tens of thousands of free tickets to White Stockings games along with any purchase, exaggerated ticket sales to impress the newspapers (his club secretary later admitted to doubling and tripling the attendance figures he gave the newspapers), and also loaned John Day, owner of the troubled Giants, enough money to stay in business and combat the Players' League in New York. Spalding's efforts worked on all fronts. Unable to earn the money it needed or draw the crowds it wanted, the Players' League folded after one season, and the players returned to their National League teams (they did, however, get the salary concessions they had sought). The White Stockings and most National League teams survived the war with the Players' League, but the American Association did not. Its teams were hurt so badly by the Players' League that the entire league collapsed after the

Outfielder Jimmy Ryan, pictured here on an 1888 cigarette card, arrived in Chicago in the spring of 1886, hit .306 for the season, and helped lead Chicago to another pennant. Ryan, the team's practical joker, was a consistent power hitter who hit .309 over an eighteen-year career.

1891 season; the four strongest teams were absorbed into the National League, making it a twelve-team circuit (it would shrink back to eight teams in 1900).

The White Stockings were weakened by the Players' League war. By the early 1890s many of their top players were getting older and the competition in the new, larger circuit was tougher. The team changed its name to the Colts in 1893 and then to the Orphans when Anson was fired in 1897, but that did little

OLD JUDGE CIGARETTES Goodwin & Co., New York.

JAMES RYAN.
CENTRE FIELDER - CHICAGO.

Bill Hutchinson, pictured here in another Old Judge card, gave the majors a dose of respectability when he joined Chicago in 1889, direct from the campus of Yale University.

The Chicago White Stockings knew how to dress up for a photo session. Here, the 1888 team, which finished third in the National League, poses for Joseph Hall of Brooklyn. Half are wearing their Sunday finest, and half their uniforms with a sports coat, with flower in lapel, tossed over them.

In 1900 kids could rearrange the ceramic tiles in this little box to put together any week's standings in the National League.

good. A new round of player thefts, with the advent in 1901 of the rival American League, further decimated the team. Starting in 1871 the White Stockings had had a remarkable run, winning six pen-

nants and creating a passionate following among the hardworking people of Chicago. Now, as the new century began with fifth-, sixth-, and fifth-place finishes from 1900 to 1902, the team was foundering.

CHAPTER TWO

A NEW NAME, A NEW AGE

1902 TO 1916

The new century howled into America. Feisty Theodore Roosevelt was president, the Wild West had been settled, the Spanish-American War had been won. Chicago boomed: The city's population was over one million and there were four hundred buildings over ten stories high.

Over at the West Side Grounds, the new century didn't begin until 1902, when two things of note happened. First, sportswriters began to call the team the Cubs because of the unusual number of young players they had to use in the wake of American League roster raids (which continued until the leagues declared a truce in 1903). Second, shortstop Joe Tinker and second baseman Johnny Evers arrived. They hooked up with first baseman Frank Chance, a regular since 1898, to form the most legendary double-play combination in history, popularized in Franklin P. Adams's poem.

Chance, known as the "Peerless Leader," became one of the game's youngest player-managers in the middle of the 1905 season, and the club climbed to third place. The stage was set for the 1906 season, a year that would begin the team's second great age.

The Cubs played their games at the West Side Grounds, a two-tiered, ten-thousand-seat wooden ballpark. Its large playing field was

Nobody had more nicknames than Mordecai Brown. He was nicknamed Miner because as a teenager he worked in a mine. He also picked up the nickname Three-Finger because he lost one and a half fingers and mangled another in a farm accident when he was a boy. The strange configuration of fingers enabled him to throw a curve ball that broke several feet. Three-Finger Brown won twenty games six years in a row, with a high of twenty-nine in 1908, in leading the Cubs to four pennants.

35

The Cubs made beautiful music together in the early 1900s, and so did fans who played this Cubs harmonica, with its sweeping script letters.

From about 1906 on, clubs produced commemorative bats. This 1907 bat honors the team, which took the World Series, and player-manager Frank Chance.

Bazooka Gum used the Cubs in advertising their famous "blony" gum in 1906.

This unusual "mail card" could be sent to friends. It folded out in six pages to display fifteen pictures of ballplayers and a game scorecard. This one was mailed to a fan in 1908.

surrounded by high wooden outfield walls covered with brightly colored signs advertising breweries, hotels, and laundries. Like Wrigley, it was nestled into the middle of a congested working-class neighborhood. The Cubs had loyal fans who jammed the park for home games, particularly against rivals like the Cards, Pirates, and Giants. When all the seats were sold the fans sat on the outfield grass itself for big games as they did in so many ballparks of the day. Hundreds more watched from rooftops beyond the outfield, just as fans do today. The *Chicago Tribune* of August 28, 1908, described a typical game day:

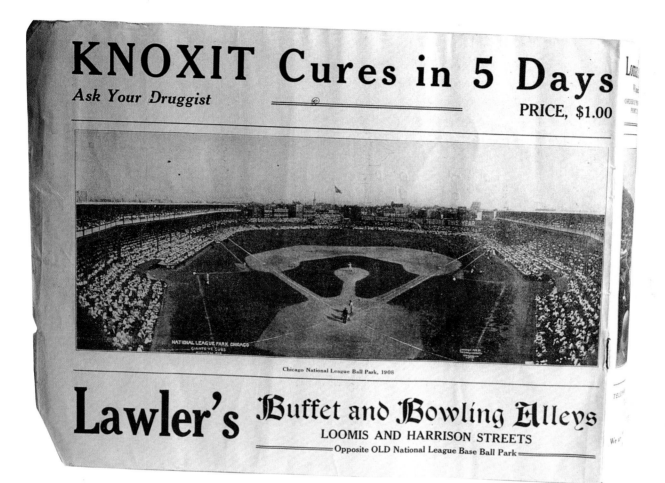

KNOXIT Cures in 5 Days

Ask Your Druggist

PRICE, $1.00

Chicago National League Ball Park, 1908

Lawler's Buffet and Bowling Alleys
LOOMIS AND HARRISON STREETS
Opposite OLD National League Base Ball Park

Two-tiered West Side Grounds was one of the busiest ballparks in America in 1908. The ballpark was home to the Cubs, the Chicago American Giants, (the sensational black team), and the teams of the semi-pro Chicago City League.

By a wide margin the largest crowd that has squeezed into the park this year saw the triumph [a 5-1 win over the Giants] and rooted themselves into a compact jam of yelping humanity. From noon until time to start the game long lines of eager patrons besieged every ticket window, and an hour before the battle was scheduled to start not another inch of space was left in the enlarged stands.

Under this tremendous pressure President Murphy's resolution to keep the field clear melted like wax in a candle flame. First an effort was made to keep the overflow on foul ground. The old lady who tried to keep back the ocean with her broom would have been an odds-on favorite in comparison. Soon the dammed-up stream burst its barrier and flowed around the entire field.

37

This souvenir pin and bat were sold around 1907. Until the 1930s, the bear cub in the logo was realistically drawn.

Fans carried small cans of chewing tobacco with them in hip pockets.

The fans had a lot to watch on Cubs teams from 1906 on. There was, of course, Tinker to Evers to Chance. Actually, they lived larger in poetry and lore than they did turning a double play on the wide infield of the West Side Grounds. In 1910, the year of Adams's whimsical poem, Tinker to Evers to Chance made only sixteen double plays.

This 1909 press pass to West Side Park, kept by a sports-writer, is still in beautiful condition.

During the years they played together, they averaged less than twenty double plays a season (actually, no other double-play combination did much better in the dead ball era). None of them was physically imposing (Chance was just five-nine), but, as fielders and batters, the three were the brilliant core of the Cubs.

The stocky, two-hundred-pound Frank Chance was a fine player who hit .297 lifetime and led the league in runs and stolen bases on several occasions. His real fame was as a tough player-manager. As the highly disciplined skipper of the Cubs for seven full seasons, he won one hundred games four times and never finished lower than third.

The slight, sallow-faced Johnny Evers was a spotty hitter. He posted only a .270 lifetime average, but in 1912 hit .341. He hit .350 in the 1907 and 1908 World

Series and, with the Boston Braves in 1914, hit .438 in that World Series. He was a gem of a second baseman, though. Called "the Crab" for his style of charging ground balls and throwing to first, he was the backup every pitcher dreamed of.

Joe Tinker played regularly for eleven consecutive years and led the league's shortstops in fielding percentage four times. He was a clutch hitter, and also a fast runner who averaged twenty-eight stolen bases a season. In 1910 he stole home twice in one game. A snappy dresser and entrepreneur, Tinker was a great hero in Chicago during that era. His face adorned the inside box top of Joe Tinker Cigars and other products. Fans and writers adored him, and the typewriters gushed whenever he did something dramatic. Take, for instance, this account of his game-winning hit on July 18, 1908, by sportswriter Charles Dryden in the *Chicago Tribune* (the "pads" he refers to are the seat cushions that fans loved to toss in celebration in Chicago and other cities):

This striking picture of Joe Tinker was taken in 1908. Preseason photos were taken in a hotel room or photo studio with an empty backdrop; players had to trudge up and down stairs in the middle of winter in their uniforms for the photo sessions.

TINKER TO EVERS TO CHANCE

Tinker, s.s. Chicago Nat'l

EVERS, CHICAGO NAT'L

CHANCE, CHICAGO NAT'L

By sheer coincidence, these three tobacco cards of the 1908 to 1910 era show the fabled double-play combination in three different styles of Cubs uniforms.

Second baseman Evers lives forever in this locket.

The bats of Joe Tinker, Johnny Evers, and Frank Chance made them good ballplayers. Their defensive skills made them great ones.

Sports columnist Franklin P. Adams made them immortals. He penned his legendary poem about the trio after Chicago thumped his Giants in 1910. The poem caught on and the trio became part of the American language, a synonym for precision teamwork.

They weren't great hitters. Tinker hit .235 lifetime and Evers .270. By today's standards they didn't actually make a lot of double plays. In 1910, the year the poem was written, they turned just sixteen of them and only averaged about twenty a year. Make no mistake, though, they were defensive titans. They played in the "dead ball" era, when the baseball was not tightly wound and did not travel great distances. Most batted balls were driven on the ground or in the air toward the infielders, not the outfielders. Downward chops and bunts were used frequently. Tinker, Evers, and Chance fielded superbly, always seemed to know where to throw, and rarely blundered. All three were consummate, all-around ballplayers.

New York sportswriter Franklin Adams penned his "Tinker to Evers to Chance" poem in 1910, and it became an instant sensation. It was reprinted in hundreds of newspapers and magazines and used with illustrations, such as this one.

Tinker, among others, appeared under the lids of Colgan's Gum Chips, a popular set in 1910.

Ironically, Tinker and Evers did not get along and got into such a violent argument over a cab fare in 1905 that they stopped talking to each other and did not speak again until the 1938 World Series, when a chance meeting brought them face to face. Poetically, Tinker, Evers, and Chance were inducted into the Hall of Fame as a trio in 1946.

Frank Chance graced this pin in 1910. Dozens of players appeared on various pin and bottle-cap sets in that era.

These are the saddest of possible words,
Tinker to Evers to Chance.
Trio of Bear Cubs and fleeter than birds,
Tinker to Evers to Chance.
Thoughtlessly pricking our gonfalon bubble,
Making a Giant hit into a double,
Words that are weighty with nothing but trouble,
Tinker to Evers to Chance.

Three-Finger Brown, tobacco firmly in cheek, peers out from this 1907 post-card sold throughout the Windy City.

After 1906, when the light hitting and lightly regarded White Sox beat the powerful Cubs in the World Series, the Chicago teams played each other every year in a post-season series.

The black pads sailed out of the stands like a shower of buzzards turned loose by dotty bugs in an effort to pay homage to the greatness of the Hero Tinker. A pass to Evers laid the fuse for the explosion. Moran whaled a double over the third base and the Cubs were in position for Mr. T to apply the match. Joseph leaned his faithful pestle against the first pitch and—bingorino! Away went the ball between left and center. McCormick and Seymour approached each other, but the bounding pill passed a given point long before they reached said point. Mac and Cy wheeled about and headed for the box stalls as Evers and Moran hustled the other way and it was all over but chucking the cushions.

While the fabled double-play combination handled the defense, the best hitters on the 1906 team were third baseman Harry Steinfeldt, at .327, and catcher Johnny Kling, at .314. But despite the presence of these great fielders and hitters, the anchor of the Cubs was the marvelously talented pitching staff. Orval Overall, Ed Reulbach, Jack Taylor, Carl Lundgren, and Three-Finger Brown: all were accomplished hurlers, and worked together for years, but the true star of the mound staff was Brown.

During a farming accident as a boy in Nyesville, Indiana, Mordecai Brown lost most of the index finger of his right hand and part of his pinky and had his middle finger grotesquely bent. Brown so baffled hitters with a sweeping curve ball that some other pitchers complained that his gnarled fingers made it easy for him to spin a curve coming off what was left of his fingers, giving him an unfair advantage. One enraged manager, hearing two pitchers tell him this, left the locker room and returned with a huge meat cleaver. "Step right up and I'll chop off two of your fingers to give you the same advantage Brown has!" he yelled. He had no takers. Whether having three fingers was a help or a handicap, Brown won twenty-six games in 1906, twenty in 1907, twenty-nine in 1908, twenty-seven in 1909,

twenty-five in 1910, and twenty-one in 1911. He retired with a remarkable 2.06 earned run average and was named to the Hall of Fame in 1949.

In 1906 the Cubs stunned all of baseball, winning 116 games (out of a 154-game schedule), still a record, and taking the pennant by 20 games. Their pitchers combined for a record thirty-two shutouts.

The 1906 World Series was not only the first for the Cubs, but the first "sub-

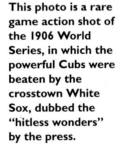

This photo is a rare game action shot of the 1906 World Series, in which the powerful Cubs were beaten by the crosstown White Sox, dubbed the "hitless wonders" by the press.

THE TRIBUNE ALWAYS MAKES A HIT WITH ITS SPORTING NEWS

This miniature bat, with the early Cubs logo, was one of many souvenirs sold at stands at the West Side Grounds in 1907.

way series" because the crosstown White Sox, in the league just five years, won the American League pennant. The Sox were called the "hitless wonders" because the team's batting average was a lowly .230, the lowest of any team in the American League. They got into the Series because in the middle of the season, in an incredible series of lucky breaks, they won nineteen games in a row. The Cubs, of course, were huge favorites with their sparkling pitching crew and hitters.

The Sox couldn't hit in the Series, but they didn't have to. Their pitching staff, which hurled in the shadow of Three-Finger Brown all year, was sensational. Nick Altrock, who won twenty games during the season, beat Brown in the opener, 2-1, with each team getting only four hits. The powerless Sox got just one hit the next day off Reulbach as the Cubs won. Ed Walsh of the Sox came right back with a two-hitter in game three and won, even though the hitless wonders produced just three runs. Three-Finger Brown redeemed himself, winning game four on a memorable one-hitter, 1-0. Then the unthinkable happened—the Sox batters woke up after a slumber that had begun the previous April. The Sox smashed eight runs in game five and game six to wrap up the Series, four games to two.

The Cubs, as shocked as the rest of baseball, roared right back in 1907, winning 107 games and taking the National League flag by 17 games. They got even with the American League by shutting out the Tigers in the World Series, four games to none, and brought a World Series banner to the West Side Grounds.

The Cubs would not have returned to the Series in 1908 were it not for a strange event on the chilly afternoon of

Sporting Life maga-
zine, the *Sports
Illustrated* of its day,
frequently ran full-
page sketches of
teams that readers
enjoyed. This one is
of the powerhouse
1907 Cubs.

September 23 at the Polo Grounds in
New York. The Giants had apparently
beaten the Cubs 2-1 on a ninth-inning single by Al Bridwell to increase their lead in
the standings over Chicago to four games.
But as the winning run scored, Fred
Merkle, the Giants' rookie running from
first base, did not touch second. Instead

"FAN THE CUBS TO VICTORY"

This Cubs cardboard
fan was one of hun-
dreds sold in all major
league ballparks so
people could cool
themselves on hot
afternoons. Both
teams' lineups were
printed on the other
side. This one is
from 1908.

CHICAGO BASE BALL CLUB OF NATIONAL LEAGUE 1907

FRANK CHANCE, MGR. & 1ST. B. CHAMPIONS FOR 1908

ALSO CHAMPIONS OF THE WORLD.

M.BROWN, P. · OVERALL, P. · FRAZER, P. · LUNDGREN, P. · PFEISTER, P.

REULBACH P. · KLING, C.

DURBIN, P. · MORAN, C.

EVERS, 2ᵒ B. · STEINFELDT, 3ᵒ B. · TINKER, S.S. · HOFMAN, SUB.

HOWARD, SUB. · SLAGLE, O.F. · CHAS. W. MURPHY PRESIDENT. · SCHECKARD, O.F. · SCHULTE, O.F.

Sporting Life PHILADELPHIA.

he ran directly to the clubhouse in center
field. As he trotted away, the delirious
capacity crowd of twenty thousand
swarmed all over the field. Johnny Evers
screamed to the umpires that Merkle did
not touch second, recovered the game
ball from the middle of the milling throng
of people in the outfield, and touched second. The umpires called Merkle out.

The fans nearly rioted; the umpires
had to be escorted off the field. The

45

Here is a souvenir of the 1908 Cubs that, when the cover is opened . . . becomes a nice collection of black-and-white photos of the Cubs.

Giants lodged a protest and put so much pressure on Harry Pulliam, National League president, that he ruled the game a draw, to be replayed only if the Cubs and Giants tied for the pennant at the end of the season (so much pressure was put on Pulliam by the Giants, the Cubs, the sportswriters, and the fans that after the season ended he killed himself). They did tie, and the Cubs then beat the Giants 4-2, with Brown pitching, at the Polo Grounds in a game watched by 25,000 fans inside the park and, police estimated, 150,000 more sitting on subway tracks, the ballpark roof, the tops of buildings, and the cliffs of Coogan's Bluff above the field, making it the largest crowd in American sports history.

The Cubs defended their world championship by beating the Tigers again, four games to one, so thoroughly beating up the Detroit team that on the final day of the Series just 6,201 fans showed up in Detroit for the game. No one knew it then, when the Cubs ruled baseball, but it was the last time the Cubs would ever win a world championship.

The world champions did not repeat in 1909 (even though the pitchers again threw 32 shutouts), but came back in 1910 to take the pennant with 104 wins. They lost the World Series to the

46

This type of perpetual motion promotional photo was popular in the 1905–20 era. In this 1909 photo Three-Finger Brown, Johnny Evers, Joe Tinker, and others cavort for the camera.

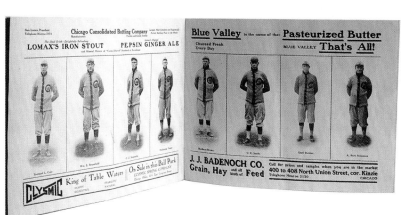

Advertisers loved to have their names and products surround ballplayers. These pages are from the scorecards for the Cubs–White Sox postseason series of 1909.

47

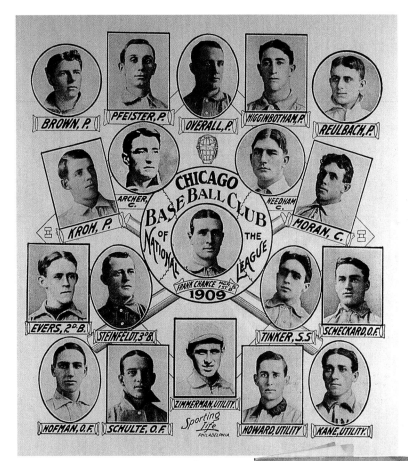

CHICAGO BASE BALL CLUB OF NATIONAL LEAGUE

FRANK CHANCE MGR & 1ST B.
1909

BROWN, P. — PFEISTER, P. — OVERALL, P. — HIGGINBOTHAM, P. — REULBACH, P.

ARCHER, C. — NEEDHAM, C.

KROH, P. — MORAN, C.

EVERS, 2D B. — STEINFELDT, 3D B. — ZIMMERMAN, UTILITY — TINKER, S.S. — SCHECKARD, O.F.

HOFMAN, O.F. — SCHULTE, O.F. — HOWARD, UTILITY — KANE, UTILITY.

Sporting Life PHILADELPHIA.

Above, *Sporting Life,* a popular sports magazine of the day, issued different team photos designed as eleven-by-fourteen-inch posters. This one shows four Hall of Famers—Tinker, Evers, Chance, and Brown.

Right, fantasy was as alive in the early century as today. This *Sporting Life* booklet, published in 1908, explained how the Cubs were going to win the championship in 1909. Wishful thinking.

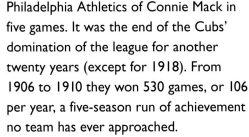

Sporting Life's BASE BALL LIBRARY

How The "Cubs" Won the World's Championship for 1909

As told in "Sporting Life." October 24, 1908

PRICE 10 CENTS
SPORTING LIFE PUBLISHING CO.
34-30 THIRD STREET.
PHILADELPHIA, PA.

Philadelphia Athletics of Connie Mack in five games. It was the end of the Cubs' domination of the league for another twenty years (except for 1918). From 1906 to 1910 they won 530 games, or 106 per year, a five-season run of achievement no team has ever approached.

The Cubs slipped to second in 1911, third in 1912 and 1913, and dropped to fourth in 1914. In 1912, Chance left the Cubs to manage the Giants. Evers became the Cubs' manager in 1913, but left after a year to play for the Boston Braves. The great team was starting to fall apart.

The deterioration was accelerated by competition from the new Federal League, which debuted in 1913. With big salaries, the Federal immediately lured Three-Finger Brown to their St. Louis franchise, then snapped up Joe Tinker for their Chicago team. This team, first called the Chi Feds, later the Whales, was owned by Charles Weeghman, who built Weeghman Park, a one-tier ballpark on the North Side. The Federal League folded after two seasons, but Weeghman stayed in baseball, purchasing the Cubs in 1916 and moving them to his ballpark, where they have played ever since. The lovely new park did much for the players' egos, but not their bats. They continued to be mired in the middle of the National

This five-by-seven-inch card displays all the players from the 1910 championship team, and, in the **middle, the team's smiling owner, former sportswriter and publicist Charlie Murphy.**

League. The great players were gone, the team's second great age was finished.

That second era came to a fitting and emotional end in one game. On September 14, 1916, the two greatest pitchers of the era, Three-Finger Brown, who had been reassigned to the Cubs after the demise of the Federal League, and Christy Mathewson, then player manager of the Reds, agreed to bow out of baseball together, pitching against each other in their final game in Chicago. The public-relations mills of both teams, seeing the classic matchup as a box office bonan-

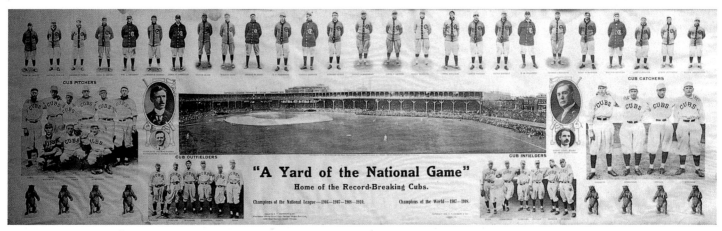

"A Yard of the National Game"
Home of the Record-Breaking Cubs.

Magnificent three-foot-long photographic posters were issued for several years from 1906 on. **This one celebrates the 1910 world champs, in uniform at the top. Fans would frame the** **posters or, most likely, tack them onto walls.**

BROWN vs. MATHEWSON
GREATEST TREAT OF THE YEAR for BASEBALL FANS

CINCINNATI, OHIO, SEPT. 1, 1916.
"YOU CAN POSITIVELY COUNT ON MY PITCHING AGAINST BROWN ON SEPT. 4th."

CHRISTY MATHEWSON,
MANAGER CINCINNATI REDS.

"THREE FINGERED" BROWN

BROWN'S TWIRLING HAND

CHRISTY MATHEWSON

CHICAGO, ILL.
"MORDECAI BROWN WILL BE READY TO BATTLE AGAINST MATHEWSON LABOR DAY."
JOE TINKER,
MANAGER CUBS.

— 1916. —

First Game at 1:30 P.M.

DOUBLE HEADER LABOR DAY
WEEGHMAN PARK

First Game at 1:30 P.M.

STARS OF MANY YEARS TO PITCH FOR CHICAGO CUBS AND CINCINNATI REDS

THE DAILY NEWS BOYS BAND WILL RENDER MUSIC

NORTH CLARK AND ADDISON STREETS.
RESERVED SEATS AT A. G. SPALDING & BROS., 28 S WABASH AVE. TEL. CEN. 448.

Three-Finger Brown and Christy Mathewson, both retiring at the end of the 1916 season, agreed to pitch against each other in the final game of their careers. Neither had much left in his arm by then, and the batters knocked them around badly. Neither would give up the ball, and they both finished the game, Mathewson winning, 10–8. As they walked off the field together the thunderous roar of the crowd for the two legends could be heard all the way across Chicago.

It was the Federals (later the Whales) of the short-lived Federal League, not the Cubs, who built Wrigley Field. It opened for the first game of the Federal League season in 1914.

za, ballyhooed the event as a one-afternoon World Series. Huge full-page ads were taken out in local papers and department stores gave away tickets to the game with purchases over a certain amount of money. Wrigley was packed for the late-season game; each pitcher was greeted with a thunderous ovation every time he took the mound. But as the day wore on, all the rainy doubleheaders and long train rides started to show on the two hurlers. They got tired fast and it showed. The hitters batted both around, but Mathewson insisted on going the distance and so did Brown. In the end, as darkness fell, the great Mathewson edged the great Brown, 10-8, in the matchup of the era.

A cuddly cubbie graces the cover of this 1916 yearbook.

CHAPTER THREE

GUM AND GLORY
1917 TO 1929

The gleaming white Wrigley Building in downtown Chicago, two blocks off the Loop, is about as far from Weeghman Park as a fan can get. Weeghman, the Cubs' ballpark, was a strictly blue-collar field in a densely populated blue-collar neighborhood. Weeghman's fans went to work on the El, dressed casually, and lived on limited budgets in small homes, row houses, or apartments.

The Wrigley Building, conversely, is one of America's most stunning architectural edifices. Rising majestically thirty stories above the Chicago River, the building is even more beautiful at night, when the glow of strategically placed exterior lights makes it a shimmering wonder. It is the home of Wrigley's gum, one of the most popular brands in the country. The slender sticks of gum, simply packaged and available for pennies all over the United States, made a multimillionaire of the company's owner, William Wrigley, Jr.

Although he was one of the city's best-dressed businessmen and arrived at work in a long town car, Wrigley was very much like the Cubs fans from the struggling blue-collar neighborhoods that surrounded the ballpark at Addison and Clark. He arrived in Chicago in 1891 with thirty-two dollars in his pocket, started off as a door-to-door soap salesman, and later built an empire with his specially manufactured Juicy Fruit and

The thousands of fans on Sheffield Street rooftops overlooking the ballpark today are nothing new. As far back as the 1929 World Series, people were sitting in bleacher seats on top of the roof to see the ball game. Note how stylishly fans dressed in those days.

This 1918 photo shows Wrigley Field with its high wall in left, but without walls anywhere else. The bleacher seats ran right down to the field.

54

Every time you take your seat at Wrigley Field, remember Charlie Weeghman. The local businessman built the park in 1914 for the Chi Feds of the Federal League.

James Leslie Vaughn's wide hips and waist won him the nickname "Hippo" early in his career.

Wrigley's Spearmint gum.

When Wrigley bought the Cubs from Weeghman and renamed the ballpark Cubs Park in the winter of 1919, he inherited a team in transition. The great players of the early century were gone; the great players of the late 1920s and 1930s weren't there yet. The team had finished fifth in 1916 and 1917, the highlight of those years having been the closest thing to a double no-hitter in baseball history, on May 2, 1917. On the mound for the Cubs was James "Hippo" Vaughn, nicknamed for his six-foot-two, 215-pound size, with the weight predominantly at the hips. He was one of the game's overlooked stars, winning twenty games five different times for the Cubs. That afternoon Vaughn threw a no-hitter against the Reds, but, in a scenario that defies mathematical possibilities, Reds' starter Fred Toney also threw a no-hitter. The teams played each other for nine scoreless innings. The Cubs then lost on a single hit and two errors in the tenth, as Toney preserved his no-hitter.

The Cubs had taken the pennant in 1918 with a team sprinkled with some veterans but made up mostly of men who stayed out of World War I with injuries, and of youngsters and minor leaguers brought up for patches of time before the

55

army called them. Fred Merkle, traded from the Giants, hit a steady .297 and shortstop Chuck Hollocher hit .316. The team had a tremendous pitching staff. Hippo Vaughn won twenty-two, and both Lefty Tyler and Claude Hendrix won nineteen. That season also brought Babe Ruth to Weeghman Park for the first time (his most legendary moment would come in Chicago years later). It was there that

Ruth, then playing for the Boston Red Sox, set his World Series pitching record of $29^2/_3$ innings, a record that stood for forty-three years. Despite a gallant pitching effort by Hippo Vaughn (he won a game and lost two by one run), the Red Sox won the world championship.

The Cubs finished third in 1919, before their sale to Wrigley that winter. The gum magnate was convinced that the

The other champions of Chicago were the Chicago American Giants, of the Negro National League, established in 1920. Rube Foster, manager and owner of the Giants since 1906, is the man in the suit in the back row of this photo. The Cubs played the Giants for the black-white championship of Chicago in 1908, after the Cubs won the World Series. They beat the Giants in three straight in front of an overflow crowd at West Side Grounds, but the scores were close.

Thousands of these banners were sold in the 1920s as the team, with Kiki Cuyler, Rogers Hornsby, Riggs Stephenson, and others, became one of the finest in the land.

Charlie Murphy returns. Yep, this is the season pass the Wrigleys gave to good old Charlie Murphy, the sports-writer who owned the Cubs during their glory years of 1906 to 1910. He died in 1931.

team would continue to be a pennant winner. He promoted the Cubs and loved the Cubs, but he couldn't help them much with their playing. With lots of money but little patience, Wrigley got rid of manager Fred Mitchell, who had taken the Cubs to the Series, after a fourth-place finish in 1920. Wrigley, eager to get back to the World Series and build his gate, brought the popular Evers back again as manager in 1921, then fired him in midseason as the Cubs wallowed in seventh place. In the years before he passed the reins of the club on to his son Philip in 1932, Wrigley would go through seven managers. In came Bill Killifer at the helm. He managed to stick with the team through 1925, but finished no better than fourth. He, too, was fired in midseason in 1925, and was replaced by Rabbit Maranville, who was fired in August to be replaced for just twenty-six games by Moon Gibson, who was then fired.

During these years Cub attendance was a woeful 550,000 a year, or just 7,000 per game—one-third of the attendance for the top clubs of the era, like the Yankees and Giants. Even the Chicago American Giants, the Negro League team that played in the old West Side Grounds, pulled in 15,000 per game.

Fans may not have had much to turn out for most of the time, but they loved to bask in the sun at Wrigley whenever veteran Grover Cleveland Alexander slowly walked to the mound and leaned his tall, angular body toward the plate. The great Hall of Famer won thirty games a year for three straight years with the Philadelphia A's (and 190 overall) before coming to Chicago in 1918. He won 16 games for the Cubs in 1919, 27 in 1920, and 22 in 1923, on his way to 128 wins for the club. Alexander had problems, though, which showed in his raspy voice and deeply lined face. An epileptic and alco-

Rogers Hornsby posed for this picture in the annual "Picture Pak" that ball teams sold to fans each April.

Hornsby, who just didn't seem to get along with anybody, came to Chicago in 1929 after years as a superstar with St.

Louis. Could he hit! A lifetime .358 hitter, Hornsby hit .380 his first season in Chicago, then .308 and .331.

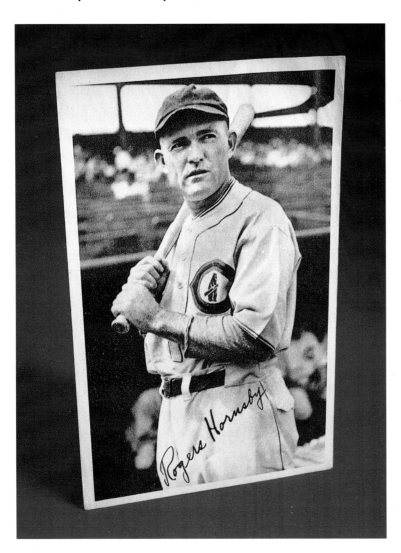

holic most of his career, he never let his troubles affect him on the field, but off it he was moody and hard to work with. He was let go midseason in 1926 by new Cubs manager Joe McCarthy. (Alexander made a heroic comeback with the Cards, winning two games in the 1926 World Series and then, in one of the game's great confrontations, striking out Tony Lazzeri with the bases loaded in the seventh game to save the Cards' championship. He was aging, though, and four years later, with 373 career wins, he was out of baseball.)

McCarthy tolerated no one's problems, no matter how legitimate they were. He was determined to build a winner, and he did. In 1926 McCarthy took the Cubs to within seven games of the pennant; they finished fourth in 1927 and third in 1928. While he had no pennant, he was carefully building a stable of powerful hitters and fine pitchers.

The Cubs boasted Rogers Hornsby, who starred for the Cards and Giants earlier in his career and was one of the game's top hitters by 1929. They had pudgy but powerful slugger Hack Wilson. Kiki Cuyler, a star with Pittsburgh, joined the Cubs in 1928. Other good hitters were Charlie (Jolly Cholly) Grimm—a good batsman and the major league's finest banjo player—Woody English, and

"KIKI"
CUYLER

Kiki Cuyler was a present from Pittsburgh. After averaging .334 there in four full seasons, he was traded to Chicago in 1928. Cuyler originally wanted a military career and attended West Point. Then he decided to work in the auto industry. A scout saw him play in a Detroit industrial league, and Cuyler quickly moved into the majors.

catching stalwart Gabby Hartnett. On the mound, they featured veteran Charlie Root, Guy Bush, and Pat Malone.

While McCarthy was changing things on the field, Wrigley was changing things off it. He renamed the ballpark Wrigley Field in 1926 (why own the team, anyway?). He started the Cubs' long tradition of discount tickets, knot-hole gangs for kids, promotions, and giveaways (the first good Cubs memorabilia was produced then), doubling attendance and, in 1927, pushing the Cubs over the million mark for the first time. One change the ballplay-

ers enjoyed was spring training in Wrigley's backyard. Wrigley owned an estate on Santa Catalina Island, twenty-six miles off the coast of southern California, where he spent his winter vacations. He had architects build a small ballpark and additional housing for his players so they could practice in one of the world's most lavish and beautiful settings.

The Cubs were thriving again and so was the city of Chicago. The town had bloomed since the turn of the century, surging in population until it was second in the United States. It had become an even

WRIGLEY FIELD

Wrigley Field is stuck in time. It is an old jewelry box, something wonderful out of the past, a stadium from simpler days, when to push away your troubles you went to the ball game. Everyone sits close to the field, a bright green expanse of natural grass.

Wrigley was built for the Whales of the Federal League, which lasted only two summers, in 1914. Owner Charles Weeghman then bought the Cubs and moved them into the park. Chewing gum king William Wrigley bought the team in 1919 and in 1926 the ballpark at Addison and Clark was renamed Wrigley Field.

Like many parks of the era, Wrigley was located in a busy city neighborhood, one block from the El, and drew a North Side crowd. It has been expanded over the years, but its turn-of-the-century architectural charm remains. The second grandstand of seats was added in 1927, more than doubling the park's capacity. The large, green manually operated center-field scoreboard was installed in 1937, and ivy was planted on the brick walls in 1938, the same year the bleachers were expanded. The controver-

Although many fans still oppose night games, there's no denying, as this picture shows, that the old ballpark is just as magical at night as during the daytime.

Actually, it was rather easy to install lights on the flat and quite serviceable roof of Wrigley. Lights were supposed to go up back in 1941, but Wrigley donated the lighting system to the army.

Who can forget this placard from the "No Lights" campaign? It didn't work. Management put up lights, but pressure from city officials at least limits the number of night games.

sial lights arrived in 1988 after a tremendous battle between fans and homeowners on one side and the Tribune Company, which bought the team in 1982, on the other.

Players will tell you it is a temperamental park. When the winds coming off Lake Michigan blow in from the outfield it is a pitcher's park, and when they blow out it becomes a hitter's park.

Wrigley has been home to World Series, in 1918, 1929, 1932, 1938, pennant battles, and All-Star Games. For most, though, Wrigley Field is not simply these great moments. It is one of the last vestiges of an innocent time in America, built before the world wars, and of a lost era of knot-hole gangs, seat cushions you tossed in the air, ladies' days, sneaking into the bleachers, real grass, neighborhoods, day baseball, and memory.

WRIGLEY FIELD

Going to Wrigley Field is not going to a baseball game, but to a special event. There's a magic to this place, the same magic that was there 50 years ago, the same magic that will be there a hundred years from now.

—DENNIS PHILLIPS, 42, CHICAGO

In the 1930s management assumed the Cubs would be in the World Series every year. They were in 1935 (right side ticket), when they lost to the Detroit Tigers. They certainly were not in 1937, when they were edged out in a single game by the Giants.

This is how far it is to straightaway center, vines and all.

You have to play the ivy on the walls. For instance, the ivy in center is much thicker than the ivy down the lines, so the ball bounces back softer in center. You have to allow for that. And you've got to watch the ball when it goes into the ivy so you don't lose it. I lost a ball in there in 1990. If they ever cut the ivy down, they'll find a hundred baseballs in there.

—ANDRE DAWSON, CENTER FIELDER

This pin, issued in 1989, celebrated the seventy-fifth anniversary of Wrigley, third oldest ballpark in America (Tiger Stadium and Fenway Park were built in 1912).

© CURT TEICH & CO., INC.
Wrigley Field, Home of the Chicago Cubs

Wrigley is a little boy's dream. It's a great old ballpark right in the middle of the neighborhood and it's filled with people who love you no matter whether you win or lose. Baseball doesn't get any better than this.

—JIM LEFEBVRE, MANAGER

A little sports history here. Curt Teich & Co. issued this postcard of Wrigley in the early 1920s. Look closely and you'll see brick outfield walls (the vines were a 1938 addition).

WRIGLEY FIELD

HOME OF THE CHICAGO CUBS

FIRST GAME PLAYED	April 20, 1916
SEATING CAPACITY	36,667
TEAM NAME	Cubs
TEAM COLORS	Royal Blue & Scarlet
ADDRESS	N. Clark & Addison Chicago, Illinois

Having the people sitting so close to you at Wrigley creates a bond between the players and the fans that you don't have anywhere else in the United States. First base is so close to the seats that I can hear people talking in the stands. It's like playing in a little town somewhere. We are their team and they are our fans. We are in this together, the fans and us.

—MARK GRACE, FIRST BASEMAN

Ouch! The first game was played there not in 1916, but in 1914, when the ballpark was built for the Whales of the Federal League.

bigger rail center, and the downtown business district had grown. People had money; the entertainment and nightclub industries boomed (despite Prohibition). Chicago's Al Capone, who ruled the town with a steel grip, had become the most publicized gangster in America. Business was better than ever and, as the Roaring Twenties ended, despite all the changes in Chicago, life was good.

All these changes certainly helped. McCarthy had assembled one of the finest teams in baseball, and the Cubs roared out of the gate in 1929. The club played well in April and better in May. By midsummer they were beating everybody and beating them badly. They came into Brooklyn and not only beat the Dodgers, but beat them four straight. They took the train to St. Louis and swept the Cardinals.

The Cubs had a solid mound staff, but it was an absolutely menacing lineup that won them the pennant that year. All three outfielders—Riggs Stephenson, Hack Wilson, and Kiki Cuyler—had over 100 runs batted in, the only time in major league history that has happened. And Rogers Hornsby, just arrived that spring, had 149 RBIs paired with a sizzling .380 batting average. Cuyler hit .360, Grimm .298, and Woody English .276. The team batting average was .303, one of the highest in major league history.

The lineup was feared in every city in the National League. Wilson, who hit thirty-one homers in 1928, thirty in 1927, and twenty-one in 1926, along with a total of 358 RBIs, was referred to by the *New York Daily News* as "Kayo Hack Wilson, master of the punch sporific." Pittsburgh writers and fans bemoaned the loss of their own former hero Cuyler, who regularly came to town to beat them now and would go on to pile up season after season of

It seemed like everyone in Chicago sported one of these lapel buttons following the 1929 season.

The Cubs issued this commemorative plate to honor their 1929 champs.

imposing statistics in Chicago (he would become one of the game's top base stealers, too). Stephenson was one of the game's most unrewarded players. Although a poor fielder, he was a great hitter, with .319 or better in twelve of his fourteen major league seasons. He compiled one of the game's highest averages,

.336, yet he never came close to Hall of Fame honors.

The 1929 Cubs won the pennant by 10½ games. Crowds at Wrigley grew week by week following an opening-day sellout. By October, 1.49 million people, a record not broken for forty years, had poured into Wrigley. They stomped their

The 1929 World Series was not one of the most dramatic of all time, but the stylish art deco programs certainly were.

Prices were steep by the time the 1929 World Series rolled around ($5.50 for this grandstand ticket).

feet, they cheered, and often they took off their straw hats (the newest fashion rage) and flung them by the thousands onto the field as the team ran off at the end of another win.

McCarthy kept counseling his players to look out for the Philadelphia A's and their managerial whiz, Connie Mack, in the World Series. Mack, who often surprised people, did just that in game one, starting sparingly used and little-regarded pitcher Howard Ehmke (just 7-2 during the season). Ehmke fanned thirteen and beat the Cubs, 3-1. Ace George Earnshaw beat the Cubs in game two, 9-3.

The Cubs fought back, taking game three behind the pitching of Bush and jumping out to an 8-0 lead by the seventh inning of game four. Then, for reasons as puzzling as the Mayan pyramids in Mexico, the team collapsed the next inning. Philadelphia scored ten runs, still a Series record, and won 10-8. The badly shaken Cubs hung on in game five, building a tentative 2-0 lead going into the ninth, but blew it, losing the game, and the Series, 3-2. Looking back, it was probably the best chance the Cubs ever had to win another Series, with perhaps their best team since the 1906–1910 era.

The stock-market crash that crushed the country later that month made less of

This late 1920s Cubs pennant shows how artists of the day were making the bear cub a little more stylized than he appeared in 1910.

In this press pin for the 1929 Series, the old-style cubbie was still being used.

William Wrigley (left) and Kenesaw Mountain Landis will live forever in Chicago sports history. Wrigley bought the Cubs in 1919 and turned them into a dynasty in the 1920s and 1930s. Landis kicked eight Chicago White Sox players out of baseball for reportedly fixing the 1919 World Series.

an impact on some Cubs fans than the loss of the 1929 World Series, but, like Cubs fans to come, they went into the dreary winter of 1929–30 optimistically. Wrigley and McCarthy had inaugurated a third great era of Cubs baseball. Fans were convinced that the engine McCarthy had built would win the pennant again and that the Cubs would be back in the Series again. They were right. If the 1930s were the golden years for baseball in America, the gold was no brighter than it was at Addison and Clark.

CHAPTER FOUR

GOOD THINGS COME IN THREES

1930 TO 1945

When Hack Wilson hit a ball, his entire body—which resembled a stuffed, rumpled burlap bag—sagged against his left leg. Stuck in the ground like a tree stump, muscles straining against the blue leggings, that thick, bulging leg anchored all of his weight and strength, creating the incredible power that slugger Wilson used when he stepped up to the plate to devastate opposing pitchers.

Hack would turn his whole body into a pitch, much like Ruth, and when he connected and sent a ball soaring toward Sheffield Street, the crowd would go wild. Hack (on his birth certificate Lewis Robert) came to the Cubs in 1926 and immediately crushed twenty-one home runs. In his six seasons with the club, he would average thirty-three homers a year and hit over .300 five times. In 1929 Wilson hit thirty-nine home runs and had 159 RBIs, but in 1930 he hit fifty-six homers and, setting a single-season record that may never be broken, 190 RBIs (his supporters always claimed he had more than sixty homers with controversial fouls and those hit in rained-out games). If anyone defined the Cubs as they headed into the 1930s—sluggers now as opposed to fielders and pitchers in 1906 to 1910—it was Hack.

But Wilson's career year in 1930 could not keep the Cubs in first. Neither could fine seasons by English (.335), Cuyler (.355), Stephenson

This photo of Hack Wilson is probably the most often published. No other picture captures the slugger's oddly shaped, pudgy body, his gritty determination, and his heaven-help-us swing as this one. Wilson (five-foot nine, 195 pounds, size eighteen shirt collar) was rejected by the Giants as not being good enough and sent down to Toledo in the minors. Cubs' scouts saw him play, felt he had potential, and signed him for just five thousand dollars.

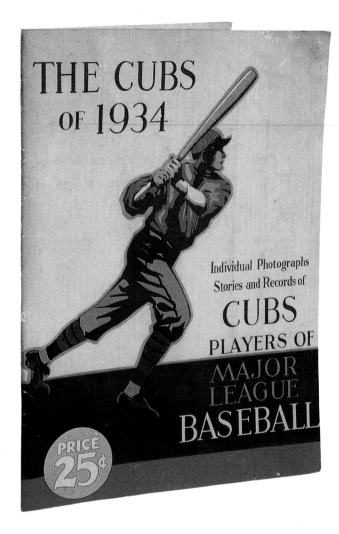

THE CUBS
OF 1934

Individual Photographs
Stories and Records of
CUBS
PLAYERS OF
MAJOR
LEAGUE
BASEBALL

PRICE
25¢

Above, one of many books and pamphlets produced about the Cubs in the glory days of the 1930s. Pages inside were crammed with photos and stats of the players.

Top right, Philip Wrigley succeeded his father as club owner. Here he's seen with one of the most popular Cubs of all time, Jolly Cholly (Charlie) Grimm. The goat's identity is unknown. So is his batting average.

Right, along with Harry Steinfeldt, outfielder **Riggs Stephenson** is one of the most overlooked ballplayers in major league history. He hit .319 or better in twelve of his fourteen seasons.

Billy Herman, his hands grinding the handle of his bat, waits his turn in the batter's box. Herman played second base in every game for the Cubs starting in 1932 and became one of the best infielders in the majors. In 1935 he led the league with 227 hits and had a .341 average. He became a staple of the Cubs lineup and played through 1941, finishing with a .304 lifetime mark.

Years ago collector Dan Knolls bought an old photo of Elwood "Woody" English in his 1933 National League All-Star shirt (that game, played in Chicago, was the first All-Star Game). Just two years ago Knolls found the actual shirt English had worn in that picture, shown here.

(.367), and Hartnett (.336), or by Showboat Fisher, who lived up to his name with a .374 mark in ninety-two games. Neither could Pat Malone's twenty wins or Charlie Root's sixteen. The team called up hard-hitting Billy Herman, who contributed immediately, but nothing could get them by St. Louis. The Cubs finished second to the Cards by two games. A fidgety and disappointed Wrigley fired the best manager he ever had, McCarthy, with one week to go in the season (a move that would haunt the Cubs in 1932 and 1938) and named Hornsby the skipper. He couldn't win the flag either, finishing third in 1931. He finally did get the Cubs into first in the middle of the 1932 season, when the team acquired hard-hitting Billy Herman, but was fired after he had severe disagreements with the new club president, Bill Veeck, Sr. That same summer, William Wrigley retired and turned over the ownership of the Cubs to his son, Philip, who was as obsessed about winning as his father. After he let Hornsby go, Philip Wrigley went looking for another fan favorite to manage the team; he had to look no further than first base, home of Jolly Cholly Grimm, the ace banjo player. Grimm, who was well liked by the players, led the Cubs to a 37-20 record in July and August, brought them back to first, and

Jolly Cholly Grimm, a fine 1930s player and a good manager, was as renowned for his banjo playing as his play calling.

Charlie Grimm, three time skipper of the Cubs, was one of the most popular figures in Chicago sports history, as these pieces of memorabilia attest.

won a pennant. Just before the World Series, the players expressed their hatred for Hornsby by voting not to give him a nickel of the World Series money. (Players give a share to players, managers, and coaches traded to or away from the team during a World Series year—a player who arrived in July might get a half share, one who played twenty games and left a quarter share. Injured players have often been voted full shares anyway.)

The 1932 team, like the 1929 squad, seemed unbeatable, boasting four .300 hitters in the lineup and four pitchers who won fifteen or more games, led by Lon Warneke. Unfortunately for the Cubs, they had to play the truly invincible Yankees, with Babe Ruth and Lou Gehrig, in the Series. The Yanks had taken 107 games in winning their pennant by 13 games. And who was their popular and extremely competent skipper? Why,

This baseball-size metal bank was manufactured to cash in on the Cubs' pennant victory in 1932. Below, anyone who holds this bat in their hands gets the chills. The pennant-winning Cubs gave this customized bat to Mayor Anton Cermak in early October 1932. Just three weeks later he was shot and killed by an assassin trying to shoot President Franklin Roosevelt, riding next to Cermak in an open car in Chicago.

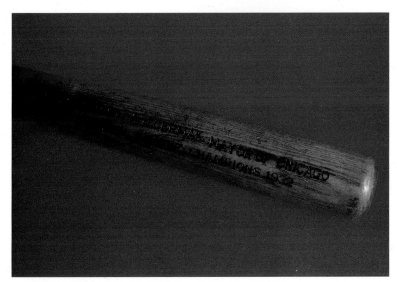

Everybody on the field had a nickname in the 1930s, so young WHO radio broadcaster Ronald Reagan called himself Dutch on the air. Reagan recreated Cubs games from teletype notes for his audience in Des Moines, Iowa. As president, he always asked his pilots to fly over Wrigley when they approached Chicago and once returned to the broadcast booth to broadcast an inning of a Cubs game.

none other than Joe McCarthy, eager for revenge.

He got it, too, and right away. The Yanks won the first game at Yankee Stadium 12-6 and game two 5-2. The Series returned to Chicago. Game three was knotted 4-4 in the fifth inning, when Ruth swaggered to the plate, his huge bat swinging like a toothpick in his big, fleshy hands. As he walked to the edge of the batter's box, a fan threw a lemon at him, which missed, and the Cubs jeered him. He took the first pitch for a strike, turned to the standing-room-only

This is **Babe Ruth** batting in the third game of the 1932 World Series. Jeered by Cubs players and the crowd when he came to bat in the fifth inning, he responded by pointing to the center-field bleachers to "call" a home run. He then hit one exactly where he pointed and, smiling smugly, trotted the bases. The "called shot" is a part of sports lore, but what fans forget is that **Lou Gehrig**, the next batter, also hit a home run.

Here it is, an actual scored program from that famous 1932 World Series game. You can see the big "HR" scratched into the card in Ruth's line box for the fifth inning.

crowd and held up a finger, indicating strike one, and pointed it toward the center-field bleachers. The Cubs players hooted at him again, as he took the next pitch for a strike and again pointed out toward the bleachers. Charlie Root threw two balls and then Ruth again pointed toward the seats as the fans began to boo. On the next pitch the Babe, with that flair for theatrics no one else could get away

Two Charlies (Grimm, top left, and Root, bottom left) were among the Cubs shown in this handy little pamphlet, small enough to fit in a fan's pocket.

with, hit a home run deep into the bleachers, exactly where he had pointed.

The fabled "called shot" deflated the Cubs. They dropped that game, the next one, and the Series. Like so many other clubs, they fell victim to Ruth.

An old saying has it that all good things come in threes. That was true for the Cubs in 1932, as they won a pennant three years after their 1929 flag. In 1935, after two third-place finishes, the Cubs won the pennant again, exactly three years later.

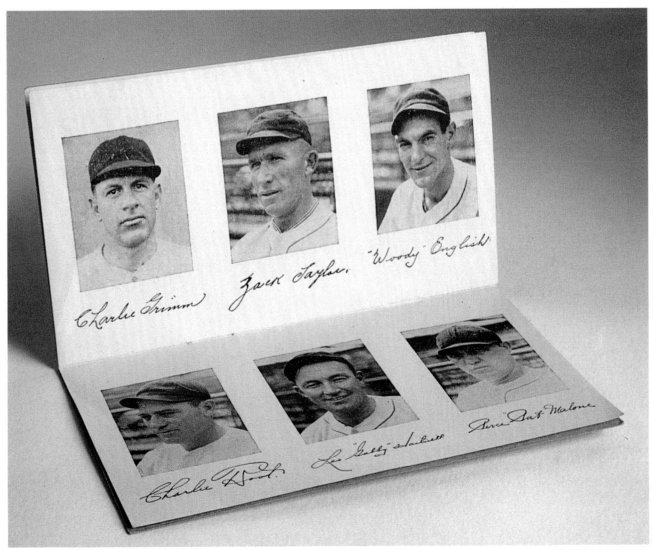

it was just one of many fine seasons. If Lou Brock in the 1960s was the Cubs' worst trade, then Gabby in the 1920s was their best find. Discovered playing ball in Worcester, Massachusetts, in the Eastern League, he was signed for just $2,500. Hartnett had broken his arm as a boy and later claimed that the pails full of stone his mother insisted he carry to rehabilitate it gave the arm its great strength. The rocket arm combined with a huge bat to earn Hartnett eventual Hall of Fame honors. He broke in with Chicago in 1924 and the

Catcher Gabby Hartnett gets a congratulatory handshake from owner Wrigley in this 1938 photo. Hartnett hit .297 lifetime and was a six time All-Star and Hall of Famer.

This eight-by-ten-inch card shows Billy Herman, one of the most popular Cubs of all time.

The 1935 team was a well-balanced squad that won 100 games. Both Lon Warneke, the "Arkansas Hummingbird," and Bill Lee won twenty games. Stan Hack hit .311, Chuck Klein hit .293, and Frank Demaree, .325.

The two most productive Cubs that year, as in most years, were catcher Gabby Hartnett and second baseman Billy Herman. Hartnett, a quiet man, somehow picked up his nickname "Gabby" with fans but was called by his real name, Leo, by players. He was league MVP that year, but

The Cubs won yet another pennant in 1935, their fourth in nine years. The heart of the order was Billy Herman, Kiki Cuyler, and Gabby Hartnett, seated next to each other in the bottom row, far left.

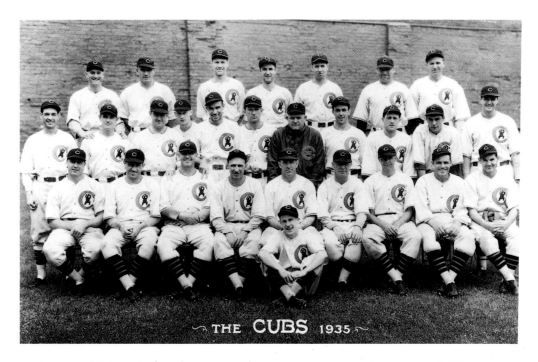

THE CUBS 1935

next season hit twenty-four home runs. In 1930 he hit .339 with thirty-seven homers and 122 RBIs. As the Cubs were winning the pennant in 1935, Gabby, who would hit .297 lifetime, was batting a sizzling .344.

Herman had a sensational year in 1935, one of many. That year he hit .341, scored 113 runs, and led the league in hits with 227. Herman came up in 1932 and played for the Cubs for eleven years, making the All-Star team ten times and hitting an impressive .433 in those contests. He wound up with a .304 average and was a dependable clutch hitter. As a fielder, he was one of the best in the game, leading all National League second basemen in

putouts seven times and in fielding average three times.

Once again, fate was not kind to the Cubs in the World Series, this time against the Tigers. The teams split the first two games, but the Tigers, led by Hank Greenberg and Charlie Behringer, squeaked out a one-run victory in game three with a come-from-behind finish in the ninth (something always happened to the Cubs). The Tigers again won by a single run in game four. Chicago did win game five, but lost game six, and the Series, 4-3 in the final inning.

By now, Cubs fans knew better than to "wait till next year." The rallying cry

Right, the White Sox had faded by the time of the 1936 postseason series, but the Cubs were still strong.

This 1933 program featured a strong Cubs team, with Kiki Cuyler, Riggs Stephenson, and Gabby Hartnett. The squad finished third behind New York and Pittsburgh.

seemed to be "Wait three years." The Cubbies' three-year turn came again in 1938. Stan Hack hit .320 and Carl Reynolds hit .302. Bill Lee again won more than twenty games (22). The great Cardinal pitcher Dizzy Dean, seriously injured in 1937 and still not at 100 percent, was added to the mound staff and somehow went 7-1 with a 1.80 ERA. Sure enough, they won the pennant again; this one would come on the final weekend of the season against Pittsburgh.

By September Grimm, in second place—not a place to be with the Wrigleys—had been fired. Fans fumed, but

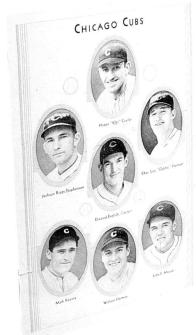

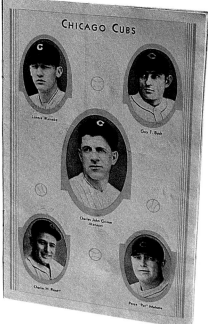

at least another of their favorites, Gabby Hartnett, was named player-manager.

The Cubs played well. They played so well that they went into the final weekend of the season with a seven-game win streak and raised fevers on the North Side by actually pulling to within one game of Pittsburgh. By September 28, though, the Pirates were so confident that they would take the pennant that they had printed their World Series tickets and built an addition to their press box to handle the crush of writers expected for the World Series.

On the weekend of the twenty-eighth, the Pirates were in Wrigley, where they fell to Dizzy Dean, 2-1. They battled the Cubs, now on an eight-game winning streak, to a 5-5 tie after eight innings that had taken a slow three hours. Then that old bugaboo, late-afternoon darkness,

reared its head and the umpires told both managers that if the game was not won in nine innings it would be called because of darkness. The Pirates did not score and it looked like the Cubs would not, either. Then, with two out and few able even to see the ball as the sun dipped out of sight, Gabby Hartnett, with two strikes on him, hit a towering home run over the left field wall to win it (it was known forever as the

Catcher Gabby Hartnett crosses the plate after hitting his historic "Homer in the gloamin'" on September 28, 1938. The final inning shot over the left field wall won the pennant after a tight race.

The ladies and gentlemen of the press (well, in the 1930s they were only the gentlemen of the press) are represented here. Press box ticket stubs rest with a photographer's pass and press pins on a catcher's vest.

"Homer in the gloamin' "). He was surrounded by each of the four million fans who later swore they were there as he crossed the plate. The rolling Cubs hammered the Pirates the next day, 10-1, and took the pennant.

It seemed like everybody in Chicago was either at that penultimate game—in the park or watching it from the rooftops beyond—or else listened to it on the radio, in bars, or at home. For some, listening to it was a never-to-be-forgotten experience. One such fan was Emil Kochlefl (eight at the time), who had been trying to construct his own radio for several weeks, without much success. "That day I worked frantically for hours to make it work," he recalled, "but all I ever got was static. That was the most important game of the season and I couldn't get it on radio. I fiddled with it some more and suddenly, clear as a bell, I hear, 'and Hartnett is in the batter's box.' Then a minute later he hit the home run. I just couldn't believe that I got the radio going just in time to hear that home run."

Unfortunately, the Cubbies once again had to play McCarthy's Yankees in the Series. Ruth was gone, but Gehrig was still there and young Joe DiMaggio picked up where Ruth had left off, hitting .346 with forty-six home runs that year. The

From the mid-1930s through the mid-1950s, artists gave the Cubs wonderful program and yearbook covers. Collections of Cubs programs from this era are among the most valued in the field.

eighty-eight games in 1938. He would appear in ninety-seven in 1939 and hit .278, then .266 in only thirty-seven games the next year, before being traded to the Giants for one final season. Billy Herman would stay strong, hitting .307 in 1939 and .292 in 1940, but, unable to get along with new manager Jimmie Wilson, he would be traded to Brooklyn after the 1941 season. Bill Lee, so effective in the 1930s, would slump to 7-19 in 1940 and 8-14 in 1941. The team would founder in 1939, finishing fourth, and fall apart in 1940, finishing fifth and 25½ games out, then sixth in 1941 and 1942.

Cubs had some good hitters, too, but they were no match for the Yankee juggernaut, which would roll to four consecutive World Series.

The Cubs held their own in game one, losing just 3-1, but in game two a DiMaggio homer late in the game sent them reeling, 6-3. The Yanks won the next two games, by 5-2 and 8-3 scores, and swept the Cubs. It was a painful loss for the fans, who perhaps sensed there wasn't much time left for this group. The old guard was getting slow, despite the pennant. The great Hartnett appeared in only

Bill Lee was one of many players who graced buttons attached to team pennants. As you can see from the fingers on the baseball glove it adorns, the pennant was tiny.

All of Chicago went wild on Charlie Root Day, August 10, 1941. Charlie's uniform, glove, and bat, a ball signed by him, plus a World Series program, and a set of Wrigley seats, all sit gently on a prime piece of sports memorabilia—an official Charlie Root Day rug. Root was a very popular pitcher, but he'll always be remembered for serving up the "called shot" home run ball to Babe Ruth in the 1932 World Series.

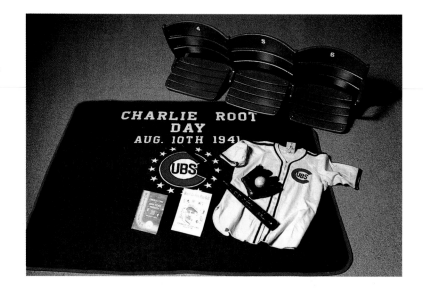

There would be one more glory year, for a quite different squad in the war year of 1945, but 1938 was the actual end of the third great age of the Cubs. They had won four pennants in a ten-year span, dominating the league like no other team since the Giants of the early 1920s, and yet there was not one World Series ring to show for it.

These three 1942 ticket stubs show the actual size of the Cubs pennant that slipped around pencils.

The Cubs were always deeply involved in local baseball. The team presented these pins to city all-stars in 1939.

The Cubs collapsed in the late 1940s and did badly in the 1950s because the front office abandoned all its efforts in the farm system. We were so good for so long in the 1920s and 1930s that the bosses just thought we'd roll along forever. By 1947 we had dried up and there was no one in the minors to bring up. That's what killed us.

—PHIL CAVARRETTA, MANAGER

During the poor seasons of the early 1940s Philip Wrigley, needless to say, fired a few managers; in the waning weeks of 1944 he brought back good old Charlie Grimm, still a well-liked figure in Chicago.

Grimm did the improbable in 1945. He took a team with no real talent and no real purpose and molded it into a champion. None of the teams had many good players in the war years. The top talent was off in Europe or the Pacific. Most teams had college kids, players with kids, or players classified 4-F. Grimm did have some good players, though, like popular first baseman Phil Cavarretta (a native

Chicagoan), who finally caught fire and hit .355, a figure that led the NL. Stan Hack was still around and he batted .323. Young Andy Pafko managed .298, and Peanuts Lowrey .283. On the mound, Grimm had Hank Wyse, who won 22; Claude Passeau, with 17 wins; Paul Derringer, with 16; and marvelous Hank Borowy, who came to the Cubs in mid-July and went 11-2 for them.

The team took the pennant by three games. Chicago fans, as delighted to be in another World Series as they were that the war was finally over, were certain that after all these years (37, to be exact) another championship flag would wave

Since the last National League pennant flew over Wrigley in 1945, this was the last Cubs Picture Parade that could say "Champs" on it.

over Addison and Clark, even though many observers thought this was the weakest team the Cubs had ever sent to the Series. The team was certainly not as good as any of the Cubs' great 1930s squads, but the Tigers, who took the American League flag, were perceived as weak, too. A sportswriter for the *Chicago Tribune*, matching up the lineups, wrote that he didn't think either team could win. But there are those who dispute the charge that this Series was watered down, such as Phil Cavarretta: "By October of 1945 just about everybody was back from the war and playing ball. In '44 teams were

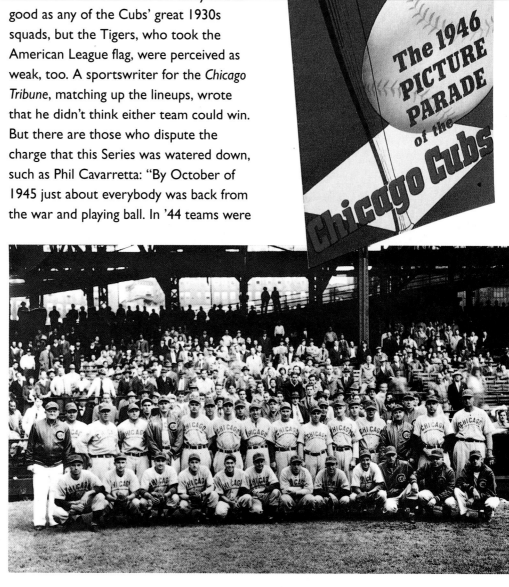

Following their 4–3 victory over Pittsburgh in 1945, which clinched the pennant, the elated Cubs posed for this photo. Phil Cavarretta, who led the league in hitting with a .355 average that year, is fourth from the right in the third row. Pitcher Hank Borowy, who came to the Cubs mid-season and was 11–2 for them, is to his right. Andy Pafko, who hit .298, is on the far left, first row.

Jack Brickhouse came to the Cubs in 1940 to do radio and added television in 1948. During his long career he also worked as the announcer for the Chicago Bears for 21 years. He was as popular as any of the players.

This primitive first baseman's mitt was used by Cubs great Phil Cavarretta in 1945. A miniature bat Phil signed sits next to it, along with a ball signed by the 1945 team. Cavarretta grew up in Chicago and joined the Cubs at the age of eighteen. He played twenty seasons for the team and was the manager from 1951 to 1953. His 197 hits in 1944 tied Stan Musial for the league lead. In 1945 he had his finest season, hitting .355 and leading the Cubs to a pennant.

depleted, yes, but not '45. Look at the Tigers in '45. They had Hank Greenberg, Rudy York, Doc Cramer in the lineup. Hal Newhouser was the best pitcher in the majors that year. He won 15. Dizzy Trout won 18 for them. They were a good baseball team and so were we."

The Cubs started out boldly in game one. With a nine-run cushion, Borowy fired a shutout. The Tigers bounced back to win game two. The Cubs mound staff did the job again in game three, with Passeau tossing a one-hitter as the Cubs won, 3-0. Detroit won games four and five; the Cubs, game six—with Borowy

Cubs danced on a World Series pin for the last time in 1945.

The Tigers' Ray Cullenbine steals second in the sixth inning of the sixth game of the 1945 World Series (Don Johnson is trying to make the tag). The Cubs won that game, 8–7, but lost the seventh, and the championship, two days later.

The last Cubs World Series pin.

In 1945 the United States won the war and the Cubs won the pennant. Many programs pushed war bonds.

These large "Gate Cards" showed fans where their seats were. Here the card sits on top of two World Series pennants and a program. The Cubs management produced the usual Series memorabilia.

shining again, winning in relief in the twelfth inning.

Grimm went to a tired Borowy to start game seven. Hank had won the opener and then pitched in the last two games. His arm was gone, and he gave up five runs in the very first inning. Derringer relieved him and did no better as the Tigers won the final game, 9-3, with Hall of Famer Hal Newhouser the winner.

It was the last time the Chicago Cubs made it to the World Series.

"I was eight years old in 1945 and my father had tickets to all the World Series games," remembers fan Jerry Pritikin. "I wanted to go very much. He said I was too young. I pleaded but it did no good. 'Look,' he said, 'Don't be upset. I'll take you next time'. . . ."

CHAPTER FIVE

"LET'S PLAY TWO"

1946 TO 1968

He leaned back ever so slightly on his right leg, gripped the bat firmly, and held it back, upright and high, waiting for the pitch.

The teenager's barnstorming all-black baseball team was in town, and several thousand spectators, black and white, had come to the local ballpark to watch them play. All the fans saw now was the thin upper body, the gentle face, and the ever-present grin of the seventeen-year-old hitter. The baggy pants of the era camouflaged the enormous, tree-trunk thighs, from where all the power came.

The body turned on the pitch, the legs driving it, fast hands moving the bat with blinding speed, and the kid hit one well over the left-field fence and trotted around the bases to a nice round of applause. It was 1948 and young Ernie Banks, a three-sport high school star, was playing for an all-black team, the Amarillo (Texas) Colts, just a year after the major leagues had been integrated. That same summer he was playing pro ball for the first time, the Chicago Cubs were mired in last place, a long fall from the World Series of 1945. Little did anyone on the all-white Cubs of 1948 realize that Ernie Banks, who would be their first black player, would become not only their best player ever and a two-time MVP, but "Mr. Cub," a man more beloved by his fans than anyone in base-ball history with the possible exception of Babe Ruth.

Ernie Banks easily cradles five bats in his huge hands as he warms up. Banks, whose large hands and tree-trunk-size legs made him one of the game's great home-run hitters, was one of the last stars to go into the majors from the Negro leagues (Kansas City Monarchs). When he came up, he told people, "I'm no home run hitter," but he smacked 512 of them.

89

As Banks spent the late 1940s playing for barnstorming black teams and, later, with the more professional and better organized Kansas City Monarchs of the Negro American League, building up his skills and power, the Cubs were disintegrating. The great stars of the 1930s were only a memory now. The team fell to third in 1946, sixth in 1947, and last in 1948 and 1949. Wrigley took out huge ads in the papers apologizing to fans. Grimm was fired.

A 1947 All-Star Game pin.

You didn't have to stand in line for three days to buy seats to see the Cubs back in 1946, when fans mailed in this season ticket card. Check out the whopping $1.80 price tag on box seats.

The free-form cover of the 1947 program contrasts nicely with the war-weary look of the 1945 program.

90

By the late 1940s, the ballpark itself had begun to appear in many souvenirs.

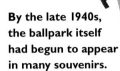

The bear cub takes on a menacing look in this 1949 decal.

Jim O'Dea, Stan Hack, Tom Casey, and these other Cubs were among hundreds of ballplayers put on matchbook covers in the early 1950s.

By the late 1940s, the transformation of the bear cub on pennants from a realistic character to a cartoon is well underway.

In one of the most prophetic paintings of all time, Norman Rockwell chose the Cubs as his model of eternal losers in this 1948 cover for the *Saturday Evening Post*.

This is one of the crispest All-Star Game tickets we've seen, even after nearly five decades. As always,

Joe DiMaggio haunted Wrigley fans in this game, tying up the 1947 All-Star classic with a double.

91

This 1950 illustration of a baseball hurtling at the reader seems almost three-dimensional.

Above, these programs from the 1952 season showcase the style of the Cubs programs from that era. Fans probably saved more of these than any others in the team's history.

Left, the happy faces of the fans reflect the sunny disposition of the Cubs in the 1950s, even though the team never won much of anything.

Above, check the way the ball leaps off the bat and the glove s-t-r-e-t-c-h-e-s out in these two gorgeous 1953 programs.

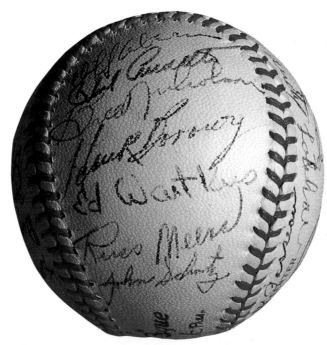

Two very mean bats. The top one belonged to Hank Sauer, one of the great power hitters in Cubs history (from 1950 to 1955, his years with the Cubs, Sauer averaged twenty-nine homers a year). The other is Phil Cavarretta's. He hit .293 lifetime and led the National League in 1945 with a .355 average.

Any collector would want this 1947 team ball with pitcher Hank Borowy's signature, but a more intriguing signature is that right below it—Eddie Waitkus. He was a promising first baseman who was shot in a hotel room by a woman he didn't know (yes, it was the inspiration for the novel and film, *The Natural*).

The Cubs did have two good players in Cavarretta, who certainly played well throughout the 1940s after leading the league in batting in 1945, and in young Andy Pafko, but no one else. The team was fifth in 1950 and stumbled back to last under new manager Frankie Frisch in 1951. He was fired. Cavarretta became player-manager. In 1952 Pafko was traded and fans fumed. The team became a target of would-be history makers. When Warren Spahn tied the all-time record of eighteen strikeouts in one game, he did it against the Cubs, of course.

There were some bright spots. Outfielder Hank Sauer did win the league MVP award in 1952, hitting thirty-seven

Big Hank Sauer toiled in the minors, unnoticed by scouts, for years before moving up to the Reds at the age of thirty-one. They traded him to the Cubs in 1949. During his first month in Chicago he hit eleven homers. He hit thirty-seven (tied for the league lead) in 1952 and won the MVP award. He hit forty-one more in 1954. He was also the first player to hit three homers in one game off the same pitcher.

home runs and 121 RBIs. Sauer, a slow runner who could hit with power to all fields, carved out a fine career in Chicago. He hit 41 homers in 1954, twice hit three home runs in one game, and finished his career with 288 home runs and 876 RBIs. In 1953 the Cubs obtained Ralph Kiner, who hit twenty-eight home runs for them that year and twenty-two the next.

They didn't help. Pitchers didn't win and hitters didn't hit. Managers came and went. By the spring of 1954, when the team brought up shortstop Banks for good, the Cubs were stuck in the second division and going nowhere. From 1945 to 1950 the team drew an average of 1.2 million fans a year, but the totals began to slip after that and throughout the 1950s they pulled just 834,000 a season, or just 10,000 a game.

The arrival of Ernie Banks was nothing special. Although he was the Cubs' first black player, the game had been integrated for seven years and more than two dozen blacks—people like Willie Mays, Jackie Robinson, Roy Campanella, Don Newcombe, Larry Doby, and Monte Irvin—were playing in the big leagues. Banks was certainly welcomed by Chicago's large black population. His first year was a good one, but nothing foretold his greatness. In the field, the new kid shortstop

Banks was embraced by all of Chicago, black and white, as soon as he arrived. The players loved him too; in the often catty off-the-field world of baseball, never is a bad word said about Banks.

But what if? What if he could have gone to the Yankees or Dodgers of the 1950s, powerhouses who would have put him in the World Series many times?

The Cubs programs from the early 1950s were some of the most stylishly produced in the history of baseball or any other sport.

The Cubs didn't go anywhere in 1954 (seventh place) but they had a fun look to all their scorecards, schedules, and programs.

was tentative, making thirty-four errors. But at the plate he hit a respectable .275 with nineteen home runs and 79 RBIs. The Ernie Banks era had begun.

The Banks saga is one of the most remarkable in baseball. Here was a guy who was clearly one of the great sluggers of all time (512 home runs) hitting on a weak team. Here was a player who won MVPs with a terrible team. Yet he still loved to play baseball. Was it a tragedy that this great player was stuck on the Cubs? Banks doesn't think so. "I never, never regretted playing for a second-division team. I never wanted to play anywhere else. I loved the Cubs and I loved Chicago." The feeling was returned;

"Mr. Cub"

People say I was never with a winner, but what is a winner? I was indeed with a winner because I made lifetime friends on my ball club. I won every time I stepped on to the grass at Wrigley Field because I had such a wonderful relationship with the Cub players, the fans and all the people of Chicago, the greatest people in the world. Not on a winner? I was on a winner all my life.

—Ernie Banks

Here's a great collection of memorabilia affordable for any Cubs fan. Banks's rookie baseball card, bottom left, is the only item here that sells for over $100.

This booklet was one of a series of biographies of great baseball stars written for kids in the late 1960s.

THE **ERNIE BANKS** STORY

BOOKLET No. 14

Only one person in all of Chicago did not want an Ernie Banks Day, and that was Ernie himself. The owners insisted, though, and he was honored in front of one of the largest crowds in Wrigley history.

As late as 1989 manufacturers were turning to Banks when they made statues of the greats.

500 HOME RUN CLUB

Even the stamp makers loved Ernie.

Ernie Banks won his "Mr. Cub" title by doing things just like this. This boy was one of many thousands who cherished his very own Banks' autograph.

walloping forty-four home runs and 117 RBIs with a .295 average. In 1956 he hit twenty-eight home runs and averaged .297. In 1957 it was forty-three homers and 102 RBIs.

Banks's production, which pleased fans and startled veteran sportswriters, didn't help the Cubs, though, as they finished sixth in 1955, last in 1956, and seventh in 1957. That year Bob Scheffing came in as skipper and the next year, the 1958 season, behind Banks's big bat and an improved pitching staff, the Cubbies got a little better.

Three pitchers had winning records: Glen Hobbie was 10-6, Don Elston was 9-8, and Bill Henry was 5-4. Right fielder Lee Walls hit .304 that summer and was joined by Al Dark (.295), Bobby Thomson (.283), and Dale Long (.271).

"I am in my sixties and I have never, not one day, thought about that," says "Mr. Cub."

Banks blossomed in the 1955 season. During spring training he kept hearing everyone tell him they had never seen a batter with such fast hands and quick wrists. His ability to get a bat around, often waiting till the last millisecond, was impressive. Yet he wasn't producing like he thought he could. The solution was not an adjustment in his swing, but an extremely light bat, which would add to his bat speed. It worked. Banks turned the National League upside down that year,

But 1958 belonged to Banks, who was finally starting to get the respect he deserved across the country. Banks hit .313 with 129 RBIs and forty-seven home runs. He won the MVP, even though his team finished fifth. The season was no fluke. In 1959, when the Cubs were again fifth, Banks again won the MVP, this time batting .304 with 143 RBIs and forty-five home runs. Although few kept track, from 1955 to 1959 Banks hit more home runs than Hank Aaron, Willie Mays, and Mickey

There was no forced exuberance for Ernie Banks in this 1960 shot. Banks, who created the "Let's Play Two" slogan, **loved the game more than any man in his generation. A gifted hitter, he won two MVP Awards and hit 512 homers.**

Mantle, all of whom got more attention than he did because they played for top teams.

But it was never just the home runs that made Banks "Mr. Cub." It was his unrelenting desire to play well, his gentleness, charm, love of children, and above all his sunny attitude in the face of so many losing seasons. ("Why be down when you can be up?" he always said.) Before particularly warm afternoon games Banks would turn to teammates in the dugout and say, "Let's play two." The phrase—so full of Banks's ability to see every day as a fresh start—became his trademark, like Ruth's "Hiya kid" and Mays's "Say hey."

"Nobody ever had the good attitude he had, not priests or ministers or rabbis," said teammate and fellow Hall of Famer Billy Williams. "We'd get killed in a doubleheader, just killed, and he'd be walking around the clubhouse with a big smile on his face pumping up the guys for the game the next day. We'd finish last or near last and on the final day of the season Ernie would be telling the writers not to worry, that we were certain to be a contender next season. He had a remarkable disposition."

Fans adored him. "In your mind, you'd like ballplayers to be just like Ernie Banks, to play well but to genuinely love the game, love the team, love the city and the people. He was a dream, just the way you'd want ballplayers to be," said Dennis Phillips of Chicago, who saw him play often.

The 1960s would see the Cubs slowly climb to respectability again, but the decade began with some questionable managerial moves. By 1960 all of Banks's heroics had done little to move Chicago up past fifth place. No pitcher had a winning record that year, although Don

Cardwell stirred a few hearts with a mid-season no-hitter. Philip Wrigley went to his old reliable, Jolly Cholly Grimm, for yet a third time. But Grimm was the skipper for a mere seventeen games before he was canned and replaced by former player and radio announcer Lou Boudreau. He fared no better, finishing seventh.

Confused and perplexed and determined to win a pennant after sixteen years of bungling, Wrigley came up with

The College of Coaches earned no advanced degrees in the National League, finishing seventh in 1961 and ninth in 1962.

100

Third Baseman Ron Santo warms up. Santo, now a broadcaster, was one of the most popular Cubs of all time. A hustler, he won five Gold Gloves and made nine All-Star teams by hitting .277 lifetime with 342 home runs. Somehow, Santo has been overlooked by Hall of Fame voters.

perhaps the most innovative, and disastrous, idea in all baseball history—the College of Coaches. He reasoned that if no one manager could do the job in the 1961 season, then four could. He named four head coaches—Vedie Himsl, Harry Craft, El Tappe, and Lou Klein—and rotated them as managers. They worked with a poor team, had little experience among them, and, quite naturally, finished seventh, losing ninety games. Wrigley tried them again, adding a fifth manager, Charlie Metro, in 1962. This time the quintet lost 103 games and finished 42¹/₂ games out of

first. If the woeful first-year Mets hadn't lost 120 games that year, the Cubs would have been in the cellar. For the team brass in the Wrigley Building downtown, twice was enough: Bob Kennedy was hired in 1963 as the team's lone manager.

But managers alone don't make contenders. The Cubs needed players to complement Banks, and they began to get them, starting June 26, 1960, when Ron Santo trotted out to third base at Wrigley for the first time.

Santo would remain at third for fourteen seasons, becoming one of the most popular players in Chicago history. He hit .251 in ninety-four games in 1960, but in 1961 he hit .284 to go with twenty-three home runs. Later in the 1960s, Santo hit thirty or more homers three years in a row and in 1964 hit a career-high .313. In 1966 he enjoyed a twenty-eight-game hitting streak, and he won five Gold Gloves in his Chicago years.

Billy Williams burst into baseball in 1961 with a .278 average, twenty-five home runs, and eighty-six RBIs to win Rookie of the Year honors. There was no letup in his fourteen-year career in Chicago (he made the Hall of Fame in 1987). He was a durable and consistent player, hitting 426 homers in his career and finishing with a .290 average. He was

101

Billy Williams was discovered by Rogers Hornsby, who knew something about hitting, in 1960. The Cubs moved Williams into their lineup in 1961, and he fulfilled Hornsby's prophecy, hitting .278 with twenty-five home runs to win the Rookie of the Year award. He hit .290 lifetime with 426 home runs.

The All-Star Game returned to Wrigley again in 1962, and the Cubs issued commemorative pins again.

always in the lineup, playing in every game for several seasons, and, from 1962 to 1970, playing in 1,117 consecutive games, a National League record (later broken by Steve Garvey). He was in the lineup so often that for nine years in a row he had 600 or more at-bats. "I was delighted to be signed by the Cubs because I idolized Ernie Banks as a teenager," said Williams. "To me, he personified baseball and to be on the team with him was a great honor. I never saw the Cubs as losers, but just a team that never quite got to the top. I played well my first year and got a lot of support from the fans. I knew I could play major league ball that year and I just kept at it year after year."

In 1962 Banks, Williams, and Santo were joined by spectacular second baseman Ken Hubbs, who hit fourteen homers and ninety-eight RBIs and batted .247.

Leo Durocher gained most of his fame as the manager of the Brooklyn Dodgers in the 1940s and New York Giants in the 1950s, but during his seven seasons in Chicago he produced some of the finest squads since the 1945 pennant winner.

Nicknamed "Hubbs of the Cubs," he was being counted on to help win a pennant. Tragically, he was killed in an airplane accident in February 1963.

Another big hope was young speedster Lou Brock, who came up in 1962 and showed potential, hitting .263. He hit .258 and stole twenty-four bases in 1963. The 1963 team played well, finishing with a winning record for the first time in years, but stayed in fifth. The 1964 season started off with the worst mistake the Cubs ever made. They traded away Brock for Cards pitcher Ernie Broglio. Brock went on to the Hall of Fame, hitting .293 and breaking Ty Cobb's all-time stolen base record on the way. Broglio posted a lackluster 4-7 record in 1964, won one game

103

These decals and
cards are examples
of interesting but
quite inexpensive
Cubs collectibles.

Fergie Jenkins rivaled Three-Finger Brown as the Cubs' greatest pitcher, but never received the accolades he deserved. Fergie won 284 games lifetime and won 20 games six years in a row for the Cubs.

Right, the arrival of Leo Durocher prompted these "Leo the Lion" buttons, but the world knew him best as "Leo the Lip."

in 1965 and two in 1966 before going down to the minors.

The Cubs were last in 1964, last in 1965. Wringing his hands over at the Wrigley Building, Phil Wrigley turned to old war-horse Leo Durocher in 1966. Feisty Leo the Lip had taken both the Dodgers and Giants to pennants in the 1940s and 1950s, so why not the Cubs in the 1960s?

In Durocher's second year, 1967, the mound staff finally caught up to the hitters with the blossoming of young Ferguson Jenkins, whom the Cubs had plucked from the Phillies the season

before. Jenkins would have a brilliant—and very long—career in baseball. The huge, six-foot-five-inch, 210-pound right-hander would win twenty games six years in a row for the Cubs. In each of his first four seasons he would strike out more than 236 batters, winding up his career with 3,192.

With Jenkins winning twenty games and Rich Nye, Joe Niekro, and Chuck Hartenstein posting winning records, while Santo hit .300, the Cubs jumped into third place. They finished third again in 1968, proving they belonged up with the big boys. Nobody is certain what Durocher did to create so much improvement on baseball's doormat ball club. Was it more attention to pitching? Better handling of the hitters? "Just old fashioned

UP WE GO WITH LEO and the CUBS

The early 1960s saw the end of one of the more stylish periods of Cubs program covers. A fan who bought this one at a doubleheader saved it.

OFFICIAL PROGRAM 10¢

CHICAGO CUBS · WRIGLEY FIELD

managing," said Durocher. Fans were elated. More than one million went to the ballpark in 1968, the most in sixteen years. Crowds improved at other parks where the Cubs were visiting. Ratings on TV and radio soared. Finally, after all those years, the team seemed to have balance between the pitching staff and the hitters and, after a total of twenty managers in the past twenty-eight years, a skipper who could win. The year 1969, Cub fanatics were certain, would be a World Series year . . . at last.

Second baseman Glenn Beckert, like Jenkins, was never given his due. Playing in the shadows of highly publicized league second basemen Bill Mazeroski, and later Joe Morgan, the hard-hitting, fine fielding Beckert always seemed to be lost in someone's shadow. He came up as a shortstop in 1965, but moved over when Ken Hubbs died. He hit .283 lifetime and was a consistent number-two hitter. A superb fielder, he made three All-Star teams and won a Gold Glove in 1968.

106

This Cubs flag appeared in the early 1970s and became a standard pennant sold for years.

By 1968 this bear-cub logo had appeared. Here he smiles from the sleeve of Randy Hundley's jersey.

Only Gabby Hartnett was a better catcher than iron-man Randy Hundley, who led the majors in games caught three straight years. He rarely took a day off and in 1968 caught 160 games, a record. Randy turned physicist/designer in 1967, developing the hinged catcher's mitt, which can be operated with just one hand, freeing the right hand for faster throwing (just about all catchers use it today). Hundley was not a great batter (.236 lifetime) but was a clutch hitter. In the 1969 pennant drive he had eighteen home runs. An injured knee slowed his career in 1971.

107

ALMOST

1969 TO 1974

illy Williams leaned against the back of the batting cage at Wrigley Field, his eyes following the flights of different baseballs hit into the outfield by the Cubs. His tall, muscular body was about twenty pounds heavier than in the years he starred for the Cubs, his waist a bit wider, his walk a bit slower, but he still looked like he could hit .300 without breaking much of a sweat. In the stands hundreds of kids were at the rail, yelling over to him for autographs. In Chicago, once a hero, always a hero. It was the summer of 1992 and Williams was reminiscing about the summer of 1969.

"The 1969 season was the best we ever had. Fergie Jenkins was terrific. The whole pitching staff was great. We had Ernie [Banks], Ron [Santo], Don Kessinger, Randy Hundley. Durocher did a good job as manager. It was certainly one of the best years I ever had. In the fourteen years I played for the Cubs, it was the best team we had," said Williams, his head shaking back and forth slowly, sadly. "And at the same time it was the worst season we ever had. We played well. We should have finished first. And we didn't. We felt bad that we lost, but we felt bad for the people, for all the fans. We just felt we let them down."

In the summer of 1969, the Cubs should have won the pennant, could have won the pennant, would have won the pennant; but it was a

In the early 1960s newspapers were filled with stories of the "bonus babies," the can't-miss future superstars the clubs were throwing sacks of money at to join them. One of the most sought after was University of Mississippi shortstop Don Kessinger, who was given twenty-five thousand dollars to sign with the Cubs in 1963. He moved into the starting lineup in 1964 and became one of the league's top fielders. He was a cog in the great 1969 team that almost won the pennant and led the league in put-outs, assists, and double plays for several years.

109

summer that broke the hearts of Cubs fans from coast to coast. The players felt something in the air as early as March. "During the first few days of spring training we felt it. Everybody was talking about how much talent we had, how 1969 was going to be our year," said Santo.

The Cubs won the opening game, barely, in a 7-6 squeaker over the Phillies. It set the tone, though, and the victories started to pile up. It was an expansion year and the National League, with twelve clubs, put the Cubs into the Eastern Division with five other clubs. After the first month of the season, the lowly Cubs were thinking about a division title in this first-ever division.

The pitching staff just got better and better as spring turned into summer. Jenkins, always underrated, would win twenty-one games; Bill Hands, twenty. Ken Holtzman would go 17-13 and Dick Selma 10-8. The hitting was superb. Williams would hit .293, Glenn Beckert .291, and Santo .289 with 123 RBIs. Banks, his career winding down a bit, would still hit .253 and contribute an important twenty-three home runs.

By the middle of June, the Cubs were still in front of the NL East. Fans were delirious. They jammed Wrigley for all the home games and set ratings

This immaculate 1968 Billy Williams jersey, one of the great prizes in Cubs memorabilia, is covered with other pieces of Williams-iana, including several baseball cards, autographed bats, and a 1969 team ball nestled in a glove.

Billy Williams signed this image sold at stands outside the ballpark in the 1960s.

110

Right, ah, the perks of public office. This season pass was given with a smile to city alderman William Cullerton just before the 1969 season. This slightly chipped mug is from that same heart-breaking season.

Below, these bats might be what Stanton Cook, chairman of the *Tribune*, wants for Christmas.

records for TV and radio when the team was on the road. Fans from 150 miles away would drive in regularly to catch games. They brought favorite banners to the ballpark, wore lucky suits, and made season scrapbooks. And, of course, they cheered Ron Santo and his clicking heels.

The Cubs won a big game in June in the bottom of the ninth on a Jim Hickman home run. After the fans mobbed the hitter, Santo ran up the third base line, jumped in the air, and clicked his heels together in joy. Pictures of it made all the television news shows and morning newspapers. "Durocher loved it and the next

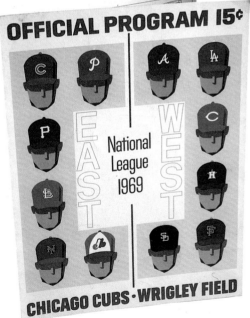

Below, this program was issued at the start of the torrid 1969 season, the first year of divisional play.

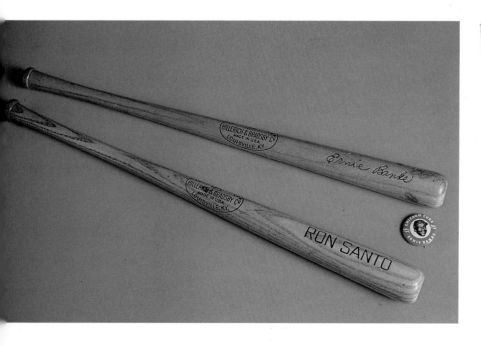

When I was a kid I understood why people always admired my father and fussed over him, because we were in Chicago. As I got older we traveled a lot and I never could get over how people all over the country would stop him and tell him how much they loved him and loved the Cubs. Everywhere my family went, big city in the East or small town in the South, we'd wind up surrounded by Cubs fans.

—TODD HUNDLEY,
SON OF CATCHER RANDY HUNDLEY

There are millions of Cubs fans who did not grow up in Chicago. Why? It's Wrigley Field. You see that great old ballpark on television—the ivy on the walls, the people on the rooftops, the bleacher bums, the old stadium—and it's everything you ever dreamed baseball could be. People love Wrigley and they love the Cubs.

—RANDY HUNDLEY

112

day told me to do it after each win," said Santo. "It became a symbol for us. Fans wouldn't leave the ballpark till I went on the field at the end of the game, jumped up, and clicked my heels. It was silly, I know, but it really got us going, pumped up the fans. I loved it."

The fans packed Wrigley that summer. Catcher Randy Hundley remembers the excitement. "We had to get to the ballpark at 10 A.M. for an afternoon game. You got out of the car or the cab and you were mobbed by fans. Inside, you'd have 25,000 people in the middle of the morning just to watch us take batting practice. It was unbelievable. I've never seen the fever sweep a city like it swept Chicago that summer."

While there was much hoopla in Chicago over the pennant that was finally ready to be hoisted up the center-field flagpole, there was more in New York, where the hapless Mets were quickly moving up in the standings. The Mets,

If there is an army of fans who think their man should be in the Hall of Fame bigger than Yankee shortstop Phil Rizzuto's, it is that of Cubs great Ron Santo. Only Williams and Banks are bigger heroes in Chicago than Santo. These mementos celebrate his marvelous fifteen-year career (.277 lifetime average, 342 home runs).

The 1969 Cubs were one of the most popular teams of all time in Chicago, even though they **lost the pennant. These huge, three-foot-square signed posters became a prized collectible.**

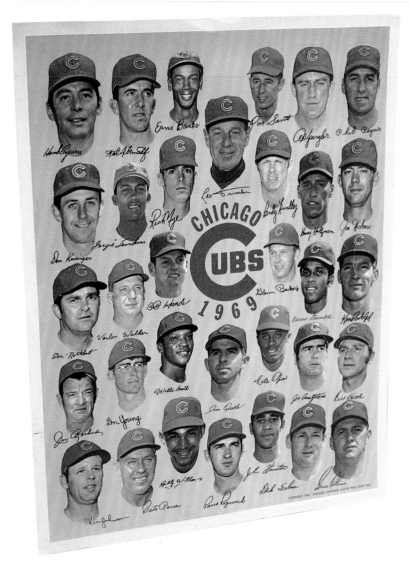

who had come into the league in 1962 as an expansion team and set a record for losses with 120, rode the arms of Jerry Koosman and Tom Seaver through the summer. They were as determined to take first as the Cubs. New York swept the Cubs in July, delivering a severe blow to their momentum. In August, with the Cubs again riding high, the Mets swept them once more, knocking the wind out of their sails and, with a seven-game swing in those two series, tilting the pennant race in their favor. By early September the Mets had slipped ahead of the Cubs and into first place. It was all downhill from there. The Cubs had climbed all the way up the side of the mountain but, once again, could not reach the top. The pitching staff faltered, and the Cubs staggered to the finish, eight games back.

The players were disappointed, but not bitter. Banks, then near the end of his career, just shrugs his shoulders when discussing the 1969 season. "There are some things that just happen in life and that was one of them. I could sit down and talk about the pitching and the hitting and the schedules and rain delays and trades and who should have been replaced when— and it doesn't make any difference, none at all. Losing that pennant was just one of those things. Planes crash. Earthquakes start. These things happen from time to time, and that summer it happened to us."

"You look at us on paper and look at the Mets and there's no comparison," said Santo. "We were a better team, played better, and should have been in the World Series. The Mets were unbeatable, though. They called them the 'Miracle Mets' and they were. You can't beat miracle teams."

Tom Seaver, who handcuffed the Cubs that year, agrees that the Mets were a team of destiny. "People talk of the Cubs' jinx and losing yet another pennant, but they forget how red hot we were in the last half of that season. The Mets won 38 of the last 49 games, which is mathematically almost impossible. I won my last ten starts and Jerry Koosman won his last nine. Nobody could have stopped us that year, nobody."

Although 1969 is remembered as one of the Cubs' best teams, the 1970 squad was actually better. That team also finished second, and by just five games.

Fergie Jenkins, the superb pitcher of the 1960s, finally did make the Hall of Fame in 1991 after numerous snubs. He had 284 victories and a startling string of six consecutive twenty-win seasons. One of his caps leans against one of his gloves (note the long fingers) in this mini collection.

Fill 'er up. Sunoco gas stations issued these player buttons in the 1970s. You got one with each purchase of gasoline.

These press passes were issued through the *Chicago Tribune* in 1971. *Tribune* execs enjoyed themselves at Wrigley so much that in 1982 they bought the team.

The Aurora National Bank sponsored this program for the 1970 edition of the long running Cubs–White Sox crosstown series.

First baseman Jim Hickman hit .315 with thirty-two homers, Glenn Beckert had another fine season, hitting .288, and Williams had his best year, hitting .322 with forty-two home runs. On the mound, Hands won eighteen, Holtzman seventeen, and Jenkins twenty-two.

The team had another fine year in 1971, finishing a respectable third. The highlight was Ernie Banks's much anticipated five-hundredth home run, coming in his very last season (his 14 was the first number the Cubs ever retired).

Fergie Jenkins again won twenty games (he was 24-13), his fifth straight twenty-win season, and finally got the recognition he deserved, winning the Cy Young Award at last. Thinking his arm was gone in 1973 (he was 14-16 that year), the Cubs foolishly traded Jenkins to Texas. Fergie pitched a one-hitter in his first start there and posted a 25-12 record, best in the American League. He spent time there and with the Red Sox before returning to Chicago in 1982 and winning fourteen games at the age of thirty-eight.

Starting in 1972 things started to deteriorate. Leo Durocher was fired in midseason as the Cubs stumbled into fourth place. His replacement, Whitey Lockman, got them back into second by season's end (Jenkins won twenty again

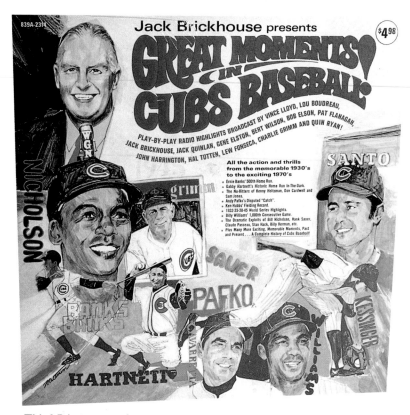

Jack Brickhouse presents

GREAT MOMENTS IN CUBS BASEBALL!

$4.98

PLAY-BY-PLAY RADIO HIGHLIGHTS BROADCAST BY VINCE LLOYD, LOU BOUDREAU,
JACK BRICKHOUSE, JACK QUINLAN, GENE ELSTON, BERT WILSON, BOB ELSON, PAT FLANAGAN,
JOHN HARRINGTON, HAL TOTTEN, LEW FONSECA, CHARLIE GRIMM AND QUIN RYAN!

All the action and thrills
from the memorable 1930's
to the exciting 1970's

• Ernie Banks' 500th Home Run.
• Gabby Hartnett's Historic Home Run In-The-Dark.
• The No-Hitters of Kenny Holtzman, Don Cardwell and
  Sam Jones.
• Andy Pafko's Disputed "Catch".
• Ken Hubbs' Fielding Record.
• 1932-35-38-45 World Series Highlights.
• Billy Williams' 1,000th Consecutive Game.
• The Dramatic Exploits of Bill Nicholson, Hank Sauer,
  Claude Passeau, Stan Hack, Billy Herman, etc.
• Plus Many More Exciting, Memorable Moments, Past
  and Present . . . A Complete History of Cubs Baseball!

This LP is treasured
not for the heroics
of the players on the
cover but for the
legendary broadcast-
ing calls of longtime
Cubs announcer
Jack Brickhouse.
"Did you hear what
Brickhouse said
last night?"

and Williams led the league in hitting with his .333 average). That was the peak for the Cubs in the 1970s. Ron Santo was traded to the White Sox in 1974, Jenkins went to Texas that same spring; Banks retired; Hands, the Cubs' chess champ, was traded to Minnesota in 1973 along with Randy Hundley. The old gang was broken up. It showed. The team slipped to fifth in 1973, then last in 1974.

August 1969 had proven to be the high-water mark for this generation of Cubs. Their September collapse is proba-bly the source of modern-day Cubs angst. After a twenty-four-year wait since the 1945 World Series, fans had wanted a flag badly; when it did not materialize in 1969, they began to assume that no matter how hard the team tried, a demon of some sort would always rise up out of the lagoon and defeat them. "Anytime we blow one, or get a bad break, or have some team sweep us, the fans remember 1969, and you shrug your shoulders and say, 'Oh, well, here they go again,' " said Bernadine Skorzewski, of Chicago.

But 1969 also cemented the players and fans together in one of the game's most joyous unions. Fans packed Wrigley that summer, 1.67 million of them, and they came back the next summer and the next and the next. The 10,000-fan attendance

This 1964 penant is one of the prettiest of all time, combining a still-evolving "cub" with the city skyline and the ballpark.

marks of the 1950s and 1960s were gone forever. Fans began to love their team, win or lose. Dan Knolls, a lifelong Cubs fan and collector, understands what it all means. "The Cubs are part of your family. They are your city's team. You don't love them because they come in first. You love them because they play great baseball, and because your father loved them, and your grandfather loved them, and his grandfather loved them."

Hamm's beer joined a long parade of advertisers on Cubs schedule covers in 1974. Hunting with a bear as your guide is not generally advised.

CHAPTER SEVEN

THE MODERN ERA

CUBS SINCE 1975

The hitter's name was Ryne Sandberg, a tall, muscular, quick second baseman reputed to be the greatest athlete to emerge from the state of Washington, where he was all-city baseball, all-city basketball, and all-state quarterback in high school. Sandberg was a decent rookie who hit .271 in 1982. He was moved from third base to second in 1983, where he fielded brilliantly but hit a modest .261. The scouts said he would get better.

The pitcher was an old war-horse named Rick Sutcliffe. He had an uneven, stubby beard that never looked right on his face and, skeptics said, made him resemble the gold miners of old California. No one in Chicago thought much of Sutcliffe when he arrived early in the 1984 season in a trade. After all, the eight-year veteran had never won many more games than he lost, and that spring was 4-5 with the Indians.

In 1984 Sandberg and Sutcliffe found themselves on a team that had been stuck in or near the National League East cellar since Watergate. Through those tough years there had been, thankfully, some fine players who had given fans some good memories. Rick Reuschel won twenty games in 1977; Bruce Sutter had thirty-seven saves in 1979 and became one of the few relievers to win a Cy Young Award. Lee Smith had twenty-nine saves and a sparkling 1.65 ERA in 1983. In 1975 new addition Bill

Ryne Sandberg broke in as a short-stop in 1982, was moved to second and became a Chicago legend. In 1983 he was named to the All-Star team and in 1984 won an MVP title. He quickly became one of the league's top hitters and fielders.

Madlock won the league batting title with a solid .354 average and then did it again in 1976 at .339. First baseman Bill Buckner and outfielder Bobby Murcer were fan favorites; Dave Kingman was not, though he smashed forty-eight home runs in 1979. However, none of these performers could hide the truth: since finishing last in 1974, the Cubs had finished fifth, fourth, fourth, third, fifth, last, last, fifth, and fifth. But that was about to change.

The scouts who had said Sandberg would improve were right. He exploded in 1984, hitting .314 with nineteen home

Ryne Sandberg (who graces a pin worn by his fans) wore this particular shirt during the stretch in 1984 when the Cubs, helped by his .314 bat, won the division title.

Dave "King Kong" Kingman, right, hit home runs wherever he went. He crashed them for the Giants for many years before he came to the Cubs and hit forty-eight in his second year with them. Later he was a prodigious home-run hitter for the Mets and the A's.

Pitcher Rick Sutcliffe, center, is hugged by teammates as the Cubs took the 1984 division title.

runs, a league-leading nineteen triples, and thirty-six doubles. He led an attack that included Gary Matthews (.291), Leon Durham (.279), Keith Moreland (.279), and Bob Dernier (.278). Ron Cey hit thirty home runs.

The skeptics who hadn't thought much of Sutcliffe were wrong. In 1984 he stunned everyone in Chicago, and in baseball, by putting together a near-perfect record of 16-1.

Riding some hot bats and the wondrous arm of Sutcliffe, the Cubs, under new manager Jim Frey, roared out of the gate in 1984, grabbed the National League East by the throat, and never let go. Sutcliffe won the Cy Young Award and Sandberg was MVP. They had charged into first place by May, and this time they stayed there, sprinting to the divisional title and giving fans the hope that a pennant was about to be raised over Wrigley—after thirty-nine long years.

The Cubs ran into a problem on their way to the pennant—the lights for Wrigley they never put up. Philip Wrigley was going to put lights up back in 1941, around the time everyone else did, but gave the equipment away to the U.S. Army when World War II started. Later, after the war, he changed his mind and decreed that the Cubs would never play at night. It

Remember the opti-
mists who printed
up the tickets for
the World Series the
Cubs never made
it to in 1937? Well,
their grandchildren
must have printed
up these, produced
for the 1984 World
Series, which the
Cubs didn't get
into either.

Remember the opti-mists who printed up the tickets for the World Series the Cubs never made it to in 1937? Well, their grandchildren must have printed up these, produced for the 1984 World Series, which the Cubs didn't get into either.

he idea that the Cubs are jinxed is just ridicu-lous. No sports team is jinxed. The Cubs are victims of some bad luck, but they are certainly not predestined never to be in the World Series again. Ever since 1984, the Cubs have had a good ball club. They have one now. I firmly believe that the best two teams in baseball make it to the World Series each October, and if the Cubs are good enough in any given year, they will get there.

**—AL HARAZIN,
GENERAL MANAGER OF THE METS**

had not proved a problem and fans loved day baseball. The Cubs were the last team playing traditional day baseball when they won the 1984 divisional title. But baseball insisted that World Series games be played at night so that more money could be wrung out of television networks, who could earn more with the much higher advertising rates of prime time. The com-missioner even said that if the Cubs won the pennant and got into the World Series their home games might have to be played in St. Louis, where there were lights. Fans were outraged.

Night baseball never became an issue though, because the Cubs ran into a big-ger problem—the San Diego Padres. In the League Championship Series they wal-loped the Padres, led by Steve Garvey and Tony Gwynn, in the first two games in Chicago, 13-0 and 4-2. No team had ever lost a best-of-five play-off after leading 2-0, but then again, this was the Cubs' first play-off. They dropped the next two in California. The final game was winnable, but Leon Durham let an easy grounder go through his legs at first and, three consec-utive singles later, the game was lost. So was the pennant. The Cubs had found another way to blow their chance.

"When the ball went through his legs you just kind of shrugged. You knew

They weren't for anyone that year. Chicago floundered with a 71-91 record and finished fifth in the division.

something would happen, that they'd blow it some way, and they did," said fan Brad Christensen.

In 1985 Sandberg hit .305, Moreland hit .307, and utility outfielder Thad Bosley hit .328, but Sutcliffe stumbled to an 8-8 record and the other pitchers were not much better. The team fell to fourth. The next year, not only was Frey taken out of the dugout (he was made general manager), but the next two managers were fired. The team was fifth. In 1987, shades of the old days, the Cubs fell all the way to last, even though Sandberg continued his torrid hitting and splendid fielding. That was the year Andre Dawson arrived and immediately belted forty-nine home runs and hit .287 to win the MVP award and become an instant star.

Different styles of cups have been sold in Chicago over the years.

Andre Dawson, a welcome addition to the Cubs family, signed both the shirt and glove.

125

These are two
schedules from a
season that was long
on nostalgia but
short on glory.

What better way
to tell time? This
1988 clock indicates
how long it is till
game time.

In 1988, the lights arrived. The
Tribune Company (owners of the *Chicago
Tribune* and WGN television and radio)
bought the Cubs in 1982; by 1988 they
were ready for night baseball. It seemed
everybody was against it. People who lived
in the ballpark neighborhood objected
because they felt night games would keep
them up until midnight or longer. Fans
were against it because they claimed it
would destroy what was traditional—that
is, *daytime*—baseball. A huge organization,
CUBS (Citizens United for Baseball and
Sunshine) was formed to fight the lights.

126

HARRY CARAY

It was just before the start of a night game at Wrigley and as Harry Caray headed up to the WGN booth, he was mobbed by autograph seekers.

"Whoa, I've got to get to work!" he said, a big smile on his face, signing autographs and posing for a few pictures.

Harry Caray, with his snowy white hair, thick glasses, and unmistakable "Holy Cow!" voice, is not only the most famous announcer in America, but is a Cubs and Chicago institution. And, just like the famous players, he even has his own restaurant.

Harry came to the Cubs only in 1982, but he broadcast games for the White Sox (1971–81) before that, becoming a Chicago fixture there. He spent 25 years as a popular announcer for the St. Louis Cardinals and many fans followed his work there because of the great Cubs-Cards rivalry.

"I think if there was a dream job this is it," Caray says. "I spend the day at the ballpark, mingle with real nice people in the press box, and thoroughly enjoy myself. I think the most fun I have is coming in and out of the ballpark, walking around the stands, just talking to people."

And the future?

"That's easy—broadcasting next year's World Series at Wrigley!" he says, and disappears through the crowd on his way to the WGN booth, signing one more program and posing for one more picture.

It often takes Harry Caray longer to walk through a crowd of well-wishers than it takes Sandberg and Grace. The popular Caray, in his second decade as WGN broadcaster for the Cubs, signs more autographs than presidents. His singing of "Take Me Out to the Ball Game" during the seventh inning stretch has become a tradition, along with his endless shouts of "Holy Cow!"

"When will I stop broadcasting games? A few years after I die," he once said.

The All-Star Game returned to Wrigley in 1990. This time the Cubs placed three players on the team: Dawson, Sandberg, and Shawon Dunston.

To drive home the point that night baseball is official despite continued howls from diehard fans, the Cubs put a photo of Wrigley at night on scorecards in 1991.

The Illinois legislature was against it, as was the Chicago City Council. The Tribune Company put the lights up anyway, but did agree to limit night games to just eighteen a year through the year 2002. The first night game at Wrigley was August 8, 1988.

The lights are still a controversy today and probably always will be. Fans are adamant about baseball the way it was.

"We were the only team with day baseball, the only one. It made us special. Now, with night games, we're just like the rest of them," said Joe Stein, manager of Sports Distributors, one of the souvenir shops outside Wrigley.

Cindy Leibach lives in the neighborhood and says night games keep it noisy until the early hours of the morning. "I don't like that. My friends still think we had a tradition with day baseball that is now dead. There's nothing to be done now. You just adapt and go on."

Ned Colletti, vice president of the Cubs, nods his head knowingly when told all of the arguments of the day baseball aficionados. "I am very sympathetic, but what about the fans who work all day and can't get to day games? What about the people who would like to go to a weekend day game but can't buy tickets because it's a sellout? We think night

Greg Maddux is the best pitcher baseball has had in twenty years. Others may have the same natural talent, but none have the gritty determination he has. This guy is just not going to lose. He's not going to let you beat him. He's the toughest pitcher I've seen since Bob Gibson. He was the engine for the Cubs when he was there.

—PHIL CAVARRETTA

baseball gives Cub fans 18 more chances to see the team."

Could the Cubs, who played 112 years in the daytime, play under the lights? They certainly could. The team now had first baseman Mark Grace and rookies Jerome Walton and Dwight Smith joining Sandberg and Dawson in the lineup for 1989. Sutcliffe was back to form (16-11), and Greg Maddux had a strong 19-12 season. Mike Bielecki went 18-7. The Cubs, now under manager Don Zimmer, played well through the summer and in August moved into first place, eventually winning the divisional title again, creating guarded euphoria along the shores of Lake Michigan.

The pennant, once again, was not to be for the beleaguered Cubs, who played very well in the NLCS against the San Francisco Giants, led by Will Clark and Kevin Mitchell, only to lose. The Cubs beat the Giants in game two, 9-5, after dropping game one. The series then shifted to San Francisco, where the Cubs continued to play well. In each of the three games there they led by a run, only to lose all three by a total of just four runs. Disheartened, the team flew back to Chicago, leaving the 1989 World Series to the Giants, the Oakland A's, and the San Francisco earthquake.

In 1992 more people attended the annual Cubs Convention than the Democratic Convention in New York.

130

The wind is the tenth man on the field. I saw [the Giants'] Matt Williams crush a ball that I knew was going to go at least 500 feet and it wound up being a routine fly to shallow center field.

—JIM LEFEBVRE, MANAGER

Players always say they get along better with a manager who played than a manager who coached, so they welcomed easygoing Jim Lefebvre with open arms when he arrived in 1992 after several marginal years with the Seattle Mariners. Lefebvre, a positive-attitude disciple, kept the Cubs around .500 during his first two years, but often slipped into third place. He played second base and third base for the Dodgers in the late 1960s, once homering from both sides of the plate in one game, and played three years in Japan before becoming a coach and then skipper.

The Cubs slipped to fourth in 1990 and 1991, but played well under Jim Lefebvre in 1992. Attendance, which reached an all-time high of nearly 2.5 million in 1989, has stayed close to that each season since. Cubs hats, bats, T-shirts, and other memorabilia are among the best-sellers from coast to coast. Two plays, *Bleacher Bums* and *The 25th Man*, have been written about them. Perhaps the best tribute of all to the heroes of the Friendly Confines came from an extremely unusual source—rock musician Richard Marx. A big Cubs fan, he made a dream music video about the Cubs winning the World Series.

You never know. . . .

There are some who say it doesn't really matter if the Cubs get into the World Series again, that the fun of baseball at Wrigley is not a World Series flag, but the green grass, the ivy, women sunning themselves in bikinis, the barbecues on the rooftops, Ronnie Woo Woo, the bleacher bums, taking your kids to the ballpark, hurrying down the steps from the El, and, well, waiting till next year.

There are others who strongly disagree. "Get back into the World Series? Hell, we'll get back into it and win it," said manager Jim Lefebvre during batting practice one summer night, his eyes looking up

over the ivy-covered outfield walls toward the already jammed bleachers. "We won't win it for the owners, for the city of Chicago, or ourselves, either. We'll win the World Series for all the good people of Chicago, all those great fans of ours, who have loved the Chicago Cubs over all these generations."

131

TWELVE
CUBS
PICTURES

BILLY WILLIAMS, Chicago Cubs

hicago Cubs

CUBS FANS

A TRADITION OF LOVE

Like every manager, Jim Lefebvre wanted to win his first game as Cubs skipper. He didn't. The Cubs played hard but lost, 2-1. Lefebvre, disappointed, went out to dinner that night and, after his food came, did little more than stare at it. "From the papers and TV, everybody knew who I was, and one by one, Cub fans came over to my table, shook my hand, and wished me good luck as the new manager. This one man told me I had managed very well that day. 'But we lost,' I told him. He smiled, shook his head and said, 'but the team played well and that's what counts.'" Lefebvre smiled at the memory. "Fans who don't mind losing? I told myself the old *Lost Horizon* movie was right, there is a Shangri-La. It is Wrigley Field."

Who are the Cubs' fans, so very different from fans everywhere else? When do they become fans and why, and how do they stay as loyal as they do to a team that usually doesn't win?

It was out of the ashes of the disastrous pennant race of 1969 that the legendary Cubs fans emerged. Something about the shared highs and lows of that season created an attitude of loving the team no matter what. Attendance stayed over a million through the 1970s and early 1980s, even though the team was usually out of the race by July in those days. Then it climbed to over two million with the divisional title of

Right through the late 1960s these photo packs sold to fans remained among the most popular pieces of memorabilia in Chicago.

133

Never mind the cuddly Cub. This bourbon decanter is one mean dude.

1984 and has stayed there ever since.

The roots of this support go back to the 1950s, when WGN-TV began broadcasting a large number of Cubs games and announcer Jack Brickhouse became as famous as any of the players. You could see the Cubs on television anywhere you went in the Midwest in those years. It helped develop a solid audience of fans who might not get to the ballpark that year, but would in the future. "The team has the great fans it does now because way back then television sowed the seeds for us," said club president Ned Colletti.

Everywhere you went in Chicago, the Cubs were on TV and everyone was watching them, even if they were watching them lose. "I didn't get to Wrigley that much as a kid, but every afternoon when I'd get home from school I'd flip on the television, WGN, and there they were. I became a devout fan in the 1960s because of TV," said fan Fred Traezenberg of Evergreen, Illinois.

In the 1980s, WGN became a cable "superstation," beaming Cubs games across the country, making millions of coast-to-coast Wrigley rooters and permitting transplanted Chicagoans to follow the team. "WGN has made the Cubs a national team, not just a regional team," said Bobby Brown, American League president.

You can tell how small these 1920s pins are by the ridges of the catcher's chest protector they rest upon.

Fans from coast to coast budget their ballpark enthusiasm in direct proportion to how well their team is doing (look at the dismal crowds the Yankees and Mets draw when they fall into the second division), but not so in Chicago. "We almost got there in 1969 and 1970, and in the 1970s and 1980s we kept coming back to see them play. It would have been nice if they played better, but it didn't matter much," said Elsie Foydl, who has been sitting in the bleachers since 1940 and has seen fifty-four Cubs teams, some good and some bad, play baseball. "When you love a team you love it, period. You don't love it because it wins. The whole trouble with the country is that they want winners. I just want the Cubs."

Kevin Sprincz, like so many fans, started going to the ballpark as a kid. He remembers how, his first summers at Wrigley, he used to tell the ticket taker at the bleachers entrance that he had accidentally dropped his ticket while buying something for his mother. The ticket taker would sigh, but let him in, only to have a string of kids follow, each with a different lost ticket story. "What you'd do when the game was over was pick up seven or eight ticket stubs off the ground and use those to get in the next seven games. The ticket guys never even looked at them.

Back in the late 1920s, the era of this souvenir toy bank and bootleg booze truck, Chicago players were always getting into trouble for having their picture taken at the rail with a guy named Al Capone.

They just smiled and let you in. Kids and old ladies. That's what made coming here so great—they wanted you here, if you paid or not. They just wanted you here."

People who live thousands of miles away from Wrigley find ways to see the team. Each summer Monte Duncan of Boise, Idaho, takes his wife, Darci, and his son, Kelly, on a pilgrimage to Chicago just to see a weekend of Cubs games. Paul Groundwater, a Chicago native who has lived in New York since 1985, is a Diehard Cubs Fan who wears his Cubbie hat and keeps score with his Cubbie pencil at every Cubs game at New York's Shea Stadium. "I don't get to Chicago any-

more," he said, "but by coming to every game here I keep a little bit of the Cubs in my heart forever."

Some fans can't limit their enthusiasm to just the city of Chicago. Hundreds of them, like Pat Fallows, go to Phoenix each March to watch spring training. "It's my vacation money. It's great fun. What else would a Cubbie fan do, spend a week's vacation lying on some beach?"

There are fans and then there are the legendary bleacher bums. At the corner of Addison and Sheffield on the morning of every game day, Bonnie Gabel sells dozens of the wildly popular bleacher bums T-shirts. Across the street, before

Personally, we prefer the fully uniformed cubbie on the left . . .

Awwww . . .

every game, the "Bleacher Preacher," Jerry Pritikin—clad in a khaki shirt and shorts and a pith helmet complete with propeller—marches around the stadium carrying a voodoo doll with the name of the day's opposing team on it and invites fans to stick pins in it. Up the street, across from Murphy's Bar, lines of people form early to get into the bleachers.

They all belong to a species of animal indigenous to the midwestern part of the United States, observed from April to September, the Cubs' bleacher bums. Since they first were spotted during the 1969 pennant race, the bums have become a part of Chicago lore, like Mrs. O'Leary's cow, Al Capone, and Tinker to Evers to Chance. They disdainfully throw back any home-run balls hit into the bleachers by opposing teams, play Frisbee with visiting players before games, sunbathe at will, bring their own instruments

to entertain the crowd, and yell like crazy for the Cubbies.

No age limit exists in the bleachers. The aforementioned Elsie Foydl, a fan since 1940 who can't remember the last time she missed a game, comes to the ballpark with friends who pile into several cars. She used to come with buddy Albert Barrett, ninety-two, but he fell and broke a leg in the summer of 1992 and doctors told him he could go to the games but had to stop driving. An enraged Barrett refused to ride in any car he couldn't drive and sat out the season. There is Carmela Hardigan, ninety-two, who goes to all eighty-one home games, taking two different buses to get there. There is Rudy Bregy, eighty-one, who retired to the

Who hasn't signed this hat?

bleachers," said Jon Mikkelson, twenty-seven, pointing to a gorgeous young woman sunbathing two rows below him.

There are the pilgrims. Each and every summer, a group of young men from Wayzata, Minnesota, arrives at Wrigley for a weekend to sit in the bleachers and watch the Cubs. "The Muslims go to Mecca, the Catholics go to the Vatican, and we go to Wrigley," said Mike Cousineau, twenty-seven, one of the group. There are the people who love the atmosphere of the bleachers. "It's just one big party with a baseball game thrown in," said Jo Buehrer, of Chicago, the object of Jon Mikkelson's binoculars.

They make lots of noise, and most of it is generated by Ronnie Woo Woo. Ronnie (real name: Ron Wickers), who leads the chants of "woo . . . woo . . ." that periodically roll over the field. "I do what I do so people can really enjoy themselves, really get into the game and have some fun," he said. Ronnie went to his first game in 1947 and was such a fan and bleacher cheerleader that in 1971 the Cubs gave him his own official uniform, which he wears every day.

Sitting in the bleachers has become such an obsession that you can no longer buy tickets on the day of the game. Season tickets to the bleachers go on sale during

bleachers in 1978. "Some people spend $800 a year playing golf in retirement," said Bregy. "Some spend $800 on payments on a boat in retirement. I retired to Wrigley Field. I pay $800 or so a year in tickets. I have made dozens of wonderful friends whom I spend three hours with eighty-one times a year. This is a perfect life."

There are the studs, the twenty-five-year-old young men who whip off their shirts and sunbathe during the game so everyone can see their muscular physiques. There are the objects of their divine adoration in the bleachers, the young women who sunbathe in bikini tops and cutoff shorts. "That's why I sit in the

the first week of March and people sleep overnight on the sidewalk outside Wrigley to buy them. The annual spring lineup has become a Chicago tradition.

"Oh, it's not bad," said bleacher bum Todd Adams, a program folded neatly and tucked under his arm. "Four of us take shifts. One stays in line, in a chaise lounge with magazines, newspapers, and coffee, and the other three sleep. Every six hours we switch off. It's actually a lot of fun."

The 1989 division title buttons were welcome additions to this collector's group of Cubs buttons over thirty years.

Would any of them trade their bleacher tickets for box seats right behind the dugout? "Never. This is our own little world out here and we love it," said Rachel Rutter, nineteen.

But does anybody care? Ballplayers constantly tell reporters they play the game in a vacuum, oblivious to the cheers or boos. Well, in Chicago, they DO care. No one appreciates the fans more than the Cubs players. Unlike most cities, the fans are part of the game in Chicago and a dramatic part of the players' lives. One of the fans' biggest fans is first baseman Mark Grace, who tells as good a story as any for capturing the Cubs fan.

"It was the first month I was with the team. The bases were loaded in the seventh and we were down by a run. I went and hit a terrible pitch and grounded into a double play that ended the inning and the rally. I grabbed my glove and trotted onto the field, head down, waiting for the boos. A double play ball with the bases loaded? They should have thrown things at me. I heard a little applause, then a lot. I looked up and there were the fans, standing up, clapping for me. They started yelling encouragement, like 'You'll do better,' 'Don't worry about it,' 'Happens to all the rookies' . . . things like that. I knew I had found someplace very special."

CUBS GREATS

CAP ANSON

How dominant a figure in Chicago at the turn of the century was Cap Anson? When he left after nineteen years as manager the newspapers and fans promptly named the team "the Orphans," abandoned by their leader. Anson played professional baseball longer than anyone except Nolan Ryan. He dropped out of Notre Dame in 1871 to play in the first season of the National Association (with Rockford, Illinois). He hit .350 in four seasons in the NA and was then recruited by Chicago owner William Hulbert to start for his first National League club in 1876.

Anson went on to lead the National League in batting three times and hit .334 lifetime while acting as player-manager. He was the star of a very successful tour of England in 1874 and, in 1888–89, a tour of the world.

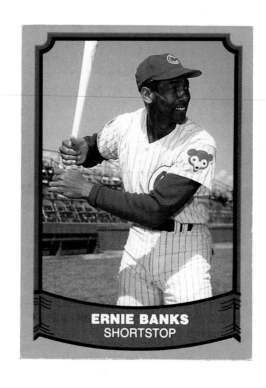

ERNIE BANKS
SHORTSTOP

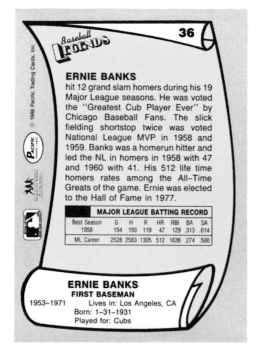

Baseball **LEGENDS** 36

ERNIE BANKS
hit 12 grand slam homers during his 19 Major League seasons. He was voted the "Greatest Cub Player Ever" by Chicago Baseball Fans. The slick fielding shortstop twice was voted National League MVP in 1958 and 1959. Banks was a homerun hitter and led the NL in homers in 1958 with 47 and 1960 with 41. His 512 life time homers rates among the All–Time Greats of the game. Ernie was elected to the Hall of Fame in 1977.

MAJOR LEAGUE BATTING RECORD							
Best Season	G	H	R	HR	RBI	BA	SA
1958	154	193	119	47	129	.313	.614
ML Career	2528	2583	1305	512	1636	.274	.500

ERNIE BANKS
FIRST BASEMAN
1953–1971   Lives in: Los Angeles, CA
Born: 1-31-1931
Played for: Cubs

© 1988 Pacific Trading Cards, Inc.

ERNIE BANKS

"Mr. Cub" so disliked baseball as a kid that his father bribed him with small change to play catch. He changed his mind. The jovial Banks, always ready for a ball game ("Let's play two!"), played for several Negro League teams before becoming the Cubs' first black player in 1954. Using an unconventionally light bat, he established himself as a star immediately, hitting forty-four home runs in 1955. Actually, between 1955 and 1960 he hit more home runs than Mantle, Aaron, Mays, or any other major leaguer. In 1958 and 1959 he was voted league MVP, the first ever from a losing team.

Ernie went on to hit 521 home runs and 1,636 RBIs to go with his .274 average and established countless team and league

140

records. He is not remembered just for his statistics, however, but also for his charming personality, his optimism that never failed despite all the losses he had to endure. "He was the most positive guy I ever met," said teammate Williams. "We'd get killed, absolutely killed, and after the game, while we're all sitting in our locker room with our heads down or kicking the wall, he'd be telling the writers how we'd sweep the Cardinals the next weekend."

Banks was the first Cub to have his number, 14, retired, and was inducted into the Hall of Fame in 1977.

THREE-FINGER BROWN

As a boy, Mordecai Centennial Brown mangled his right hand in a corn grinder and was left with just three usable fingers, one of them gnarled and crooked. He learned how to throw a wicked curve ball by holding the ball in his crooked finger and spinning it off the others. Brown became one of baseball's great pitchers, winning twenty games six years in a row and leading his team to four pennants en route to a career mark of 239-129.

His real value was as the Cubs' "money pitcher"—the one who could always be counted on to win big games. He won five World Series games for the team and, in his moment of glory, won the 1908 play-off game against the Giants after working out in New York secretly while his manager told the press he was back in Chicago, sick. Brown was a workhorse who often served as a dependable relief pitcher, picking up forty-eight saves along with his two hundred-plus wins. The pitcher's handicap was well known and he was often pointed out as a role model to handicapped children across the country. He was inducted into the Hall of Fame in 1949.

KIKI CUYLER

Born Hazen Shirley Cuyler, Kiki (pronounced "kye-kye") was a superb hitter, the anchor of the strong Pirates teams of the early 1920s, for whom in one four-year stretch he hit .354, .357, .321, and .309. He did not get along with his manager, though, and was traded to Chicago in 1928, infuriating Pirates fans.

In Chicago, Cuyler kept up his hitting barrage, batting .285 and stealing thirty-seven bases in 1928. He hit .360 and stole forty-three bases in 1929 and hit .355 the next year. He went on to hit .321 lifetime and steal 328 bases. He was a mainstay on the 1929, 1932, and 1935 pennant-winning teams and part of a dangerous batting order that included Hack Wilson, Rogers Hornsby, Gabby Hartnett, and Riggs Stephenson. He was inducted into the Hall of Fame in 1968.

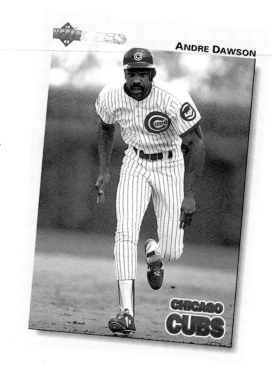

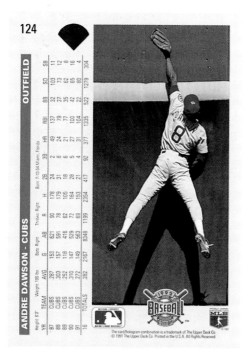

ANDRE DAWSON

The center fielder, whose bulging arms and large hands hold bats as if they were toothpicks, came to the Cubs as a bona-fide superstar in 1987. He wanted to play in Wrigley because, on legs worn down by artificial turf, he yearned for real grass. Starting out with a low salary ($500,000), he was rejuvenated by Wrigley's grass and supportive fans. Dawson hit forty-nine homers and drove in 137 runs in 1987 to take the MVP award, the first man ever to do it for a cellar squad.

His first year with the Cubs was no fluke. The consistent Dawson hit .303 in 1988 and .310 in 1990. In his first five years with Chicago he hammered 152 homers and averaged a hundred RBIs each season.

And the grass? "I love it," said Dawson. "It gave me new life. The game was meant to be played on grass."

Dawson, unable to come to contract terms with management, went to the Red Sox in 1993.

GABBY HARTNETT

He is famous for one moment, his legendary "Homer in the gloamin'," the twilight shot over the wall at Wrigley that helped win the pennant for the Cubs in 1938, but Hartnett was a fine all-around player for twenty years in the majors. Named Gabby by mischievous teammates because he was so quiet, the catcher had a rocket arm and led the league in assists six times. He became a Cubs regular in 1924 and hit .299. He hit twenty-four home runs in 1925. In 1929, for no reason, his arm went dead. Players, trainers, and doctors did not know why. His mother told him not to worry, that as soon as his wife bore their first child, the arm would return. Two weeks after the birth, the arm was as good as new.

So was the bat. Gabby hit thirty-seven home runs in 1930 to go with his .339 average. He hit .344 in 1935, when he was the National League's MVP. He was also the league's All-Star catcher six times and caught Carl Hubbell the day he struck out Ruth, Gehrig, Foxx, Simmons, and Cronin in succession. He went into the Hall of Fame in 1955.

CHARLES LEO (GABBY) HARTNETT

FERGUSON JENKINS

Fergie was, and is, an unknown superstar. Never a glamour player like Banks or Williams, he arrived in Chicago in the summer of 1966 as a reliever but was soon a starter. The fearsome Jenkins (six-foot-five, two hundred pounds) quickly became the Cubs' dominant pitcher, posting a 20-13 record in 1967. It was the first of six consecutive twenty-win seasons for Jenkins (Dizzy Dean won twenty in only four straight years). He finally received some of the accolades he deserved when he won a Cy Young Award in 1971.

Despite the six straight twenty-victory years and five seasons of two hundred-plus strikeouts, Fergie was traded to the Texas Rangers in 1974. Livid at his release, he gained some revenge by shutting out the world champion A's in a one-hitter in his first start in Texas and then won twenty-five games that season. He was later traded to the Red Sox, where he did not get along with manager Don Zimmer, and came back to the Cubbies for one last hurrah in 1982 at age thirty-eight, posting a 14-15 record before retiring. Sadly, Fergie, one of the best pitchers of the 1960s and 1970s and winner of 284 games, had to wait nine long years before getting into the Hall of Fame in 1991.

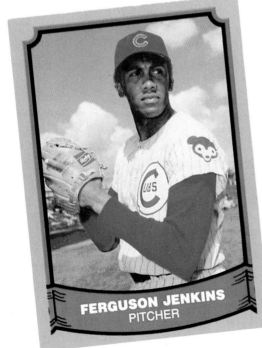

FERGUSON JENKINS
PITCHER

RYNE SANDBERG

If there is ever a "Mr. Cub II," it will be Ryno. Sandberg came up in 1982 as a third baseman, but was switched to second in 1983, where he became one of the game's premier fielders, setting numerous records for consecutive games without errors and winning Gold Gloves in his first nine seasons at second. A tall, quiet man, Sandberg has been a steady hitter for Chicago, posting a .290 average over his twelve years with the team. He has been a productive hitter, too, with forty home runs in 1990 (he'll soon become the second baseman with the most home runs in major league history). With little fanfare the fleet-footed Sandberg stole more than 360 bases in his first twelve years with the club. He was National League MVP in 1984.

"His greatness is his consistency in the field and at bat," says manager Jim Lefebvre. "Steady, steady, steady. He has bad days, but not bad weeks. He's dependable. He'll always come through when you need him."

110	RYNE SANDBERG	2B

HT: 6'2" WT: 180 BATS: RIGHT THROWS: RIGHT DRFT: PHILLIES #21-JUNE, 1978
ACQ: TRADE, 1-27-82 BORN: 9-18-59, SPOKANE, WASH. HOME: TEMPE, ARIZ.

COMPLETE MAJOR LEAGUE BATTING RECORD *(LEAGUE LEADER IN ITALICS, TIE◆)*

YR	CLUB	G	AB	R	H	2B	3B	HR	RBI	SB	SLG	BB	SO	AVG
81	PHILLIES	13	6	2	1	0	0	0	0	0	.167	0	1	.167
82	CUBS	156	635	103	172	33	5	7	54	32	.372	36	90	.271
83	CUBS	158	633	94	165	25	4	8	48	37	.351	51	79	.261
84	CUBS	156	636	114	200	36	19◆	19	84	32	.520	52	101	.314
85	CUBS	153	609	113	186	31	6	26	83	54	.504	57	97	.305
86	CUBS	154	627	68	178	28	5	14	76	34	.411	46	79	.284
87	CUBS	132	523	81	154	25	2	16	59	21	.442	59	79	.294
88	CUBS	155	618	77	163	23	8	19	69	25	.419	54	91	.264
89	CUBS	157	606	104◆	176	25	5	30	76	15	.497	59	85	.290
90	CUBS	155	615	116	188	30	3	40	100	25	.559	50	84	.306
91	CUBS	158	585	104	170	32	2	26	100	22	.485	87	89	.291
	MAJ. LEA. TOTALS	1547	6093	976	1753	288	59	205	749	297	.455	551	875	.288

Ryne hit 3-run inside-the-park HR in 1st inning and a conventional 2-run Clout in 3rd vs. Braves, 7-27-91.

© MLB & MLBPA 1992   D✹ ©1992 THE TOPPS COMPANY, INC.

ALBERT SPALDING

Not every family has a Babe Ruth autograph or Stan Musial cap, but most have something in the house connected to Albert Spalding, the Cubs' first manager who went on to found the Spalding sporting goods company.

Spalding was baseball's first great pitcher. He joined Boston's team in the first season of play in the National Association in 1871 and in five years compiled a startling 207-56 record, with 57 wins in 1875 (in those days before pitching rotations, one man would start every game for his team). He was recruited as the mound ace of the first White Stockings team in 1876; he threw a shutout in the team's first game and went on to win forty-six games that year.

His arm went after those six hard years, though, and Spalding pitched only four games in 1877. He then retired and started his sporting goods company. In his spare time as owner and president of the White Stockings from 1882 to 1891, he was a major force in the continual reorganization and success of the National League. The world tour was his idea. He was inducted into the Hall of Fame in 1939.

HARRY STEINFELDT

Who was the missing member of the Cubs infield from the Tinker to Evers to Chance poem (Chicago's favorite trivia question)? It was Harry Steinfeldt, a fine player who might have been a legend, too, if his name wasn't too long to rhyme with anything. Harry had eight good years with the Reds before his trade to the Cubs in 1906. He hit .327 that year, best on the team, and led the National League with 176 hits.

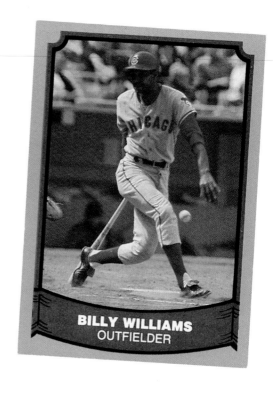

BILLY WILLIAMS
OUTFIELDER

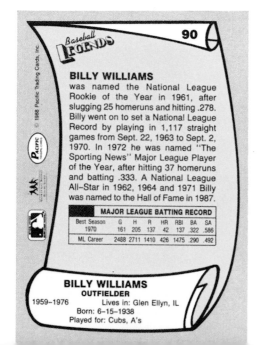

Baseball LEGENDS   90

BILLY WILLIAMS
was named the National League Rookie of the Year in 1961, after slugging 25 homeruns and hitting .278. Billy went on to set a National League Record by playing in 1,117 straight games from Sept. 22, 1963 to Sept. 2, 1970. In 1972 he was named "The Sporting News" Major League Player of the Year, after hitting 37 homeruns and batting .333. A National League All-Star in 1962, 1964 and 1971 Billy was named to the Hall of Fame in 1987.

MAJOR LEAGUE BATTING RECORD							
Best Season	G	H	R	HR	RBI	BA	SA
1970	161	205	137	42	137	.322	.586
ML Career	2488	2711	1410	426	1475	.290	.492

BILLY WILLIAMS
OUTFIELDER
1959–1976   Lives in: Glen Ellyn, IL
Born: 6-15-1938
Played for: Cubs, A's

BILLY WILLIAMS

Always overshadowed in his fourteen seasons with the Cubs by more flamboyant hitters like Mantle, Williams, Aaron, and teammate Ernie Banks, Billy Williams slowly and steadily carved out a magnificent career. He hit .290 lifetime with 426 home runs and set a number of endurance records (600 at-bats nine times, 164 games played in one season, 1,117 consecutive games played). The left-handed slugger hit more than twenty home runs and eighty-four

RBIs in thirteen consecutive years, hit five home runs in back-to-back games, crushed three homers in a single game, and once was eight for eight in a doubleheader.

Williams was Rookie of the Year in 1961 and his generous personality and the way he had with kids made him an immediate hit with fans. He was so popular the Cubs gave him a "Billy Williams Day" in 1969 and, true to form, he went five for nine in the doubleheader. Today, two numbered flags fly over the foul posts at Wrigley, a 14 for Ernie Banks and a 26 for Williams.

"I loved to play the game, but what I loved most of all was just coming to the ballpark and talking to all the kids who hang out at the rail. I'd come extra early just to go talk to them," said Williams, who was inducted into the Hall of Fame in 1987.

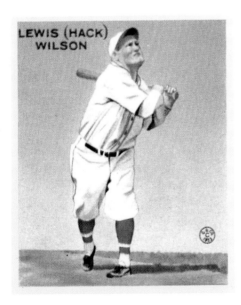

LEWIS (HACK) WILSON

HACK WILSON

Hack Wilson was only five-foot-six, but he weighed a bulky 195 pounds and had a size eighteen shirt collar. A muscular fire hydrant who swung for all he was worth, Wilson came to the Cubs in 1926 and went to work on National League pitching. He led the league in homers with twenty-one in 1926, thirty in 1927, and thirty-one in 1928. He hit thirty-nine in 1929 to help the Cubbies win the pennant and then, in 1930, stunned all of baseball by smashing fifty-six home runs (still a National League record) and collecting 190 RBIs, a major league record that may never be broken.

Alcohol problems shortened the slugger's career. He slumped in 1931 and was traded to the Dodgers and then the Phillies, where he foundered. He was out of baseball by 1935. Wilson was elected to the Hall of Fame in 1979.

CUBS STATS

Cubs All-Time Pitching Leaders (Since 1900)

GAMES		VICTORIES		STRIKEOUTS		SHUTOUTS		SAVES	
Root	605	Root	201	Jenkins	2,038	M. Brown	50	L. Smith	180
L. Smith	458	M. Brown	188	Root	1,432	Vaughn	35	Sutter	133
Elston	449	Jenkins	167	R. Reuschel	1,367	Reulbach	31	Regan	60
Bush	428	Bush	152	Vaughn	1,138	Jenkins	29	Williams	52
Jenkins	401	Vaughn	151	Rush	1,076	Overall	28	Abernathy	39
B. Lee	364	B. Lee	139	M. Brown	1,043	B. Lee	25	McDaniel	39
R. Reuschel	358	Reulbach	136	Holtzman	988	Alexander	24	Elston	32
M. Brown	346	R. Reuschel	135	Sutcliffe	909	Passeau	23	Aker	29
Rush	339	Alexander	128	Ellsworth	905	French	21	Assenmacher	25
Passeau	334	Passeau	124	Hands	900	Root	21	Tidrow	25

Career Pitching Leaders

Games	Charlie Root	605	
Games (LH)	Jim Vaughn	305	
Years	Charlie Root	16	
Games Won	Charlie Root	201	
Games Won (LH)	Jim Vaughn	151	
Games Lost	Charlie Root	156	
Games Lost (LH)	Dick Ellsworth	110	
Games Started	Fergie Jenkins	347	
Games Started (LH)	Jim Vaughn	271	
Complete Games	Mordecai Brown	206	
Complete Games (LH)	Jim Vaughn	177	
Shutouts	Mordecai Brown	50	
Shutouts (LH)	Jim Vaughn	35	
Innings Pitched	Charlie Root	3,138.0	
Innings Pitched (LH)	Jim Vaughn	2,216.0	
Lowest Earned Run Average	Mordecai Brown	1.80	
Lowest Earned Run Average (LH)	Jack Pfiester	1.86	
Strikeouts	Fergie Jenkins	2,038	
Strikeouts (LH)	Jim Vaughn	1,138	
Bases on Balls	Charlie Root	871	
Bases on Balls (LH)	Jim Vaughn	621	
Saves	Lee Smith	180	
Saves (LH)	Mitch Williams	52	
Relief Appearances	Lee Smith	453	
Relief Appearances (LH)	Willie Hernandez	312	
Relief Wins	Don Elston	46	
Relief Wins (LH)	Willie Hernandez	26	
Winning Percentage	Mordecai Brown (188–85)	.649	
Winning Percentage (LH)	Jack Pfiester (70–40)	.636	
Consecutive Games Won	Rick Sutcliffe (1984–1985)	16	

Cubs All-Time Hitting Leaders

GAMES

Banks	2,528
Anson	2,276
B. Williams	2,213
Santo	2,126
Cavarretta	1,953
Hack	1,938
Hartnett	1,926
Ryan	1,660
Kessinger	1,648
Schulte	1,564

EXTRA-BASE HITS

Banks	1,009
B. Williams	881
Santo	756
Anson	752
Hartnett	686
Ryan	603
Sandberg	552
Cavarretta	532
Nicholson	503
Hack	501

TOTAL BASES

Banks	4,706
B. Williams	4,262
Anson	4,109
Santo	3,667
Hartnett	3,079
Ryan	3,045
Hack	2,889
Sandberg	2,773
Cavarretta	2,742
Schulte	2,354

TRIPLES

Ryan	142
Anson	124
Schulte	117
Dahlen	106
Cavarretta	99
Tinker	93
Banks	90
B. Williams	87
Lange	83
Hack	81

HITS

Anson	3,041
Banks	2,583
B. Williams	2,510
Hack	2,193
Santo	2,171
Ryan	2,102
Cavarretta	1,927
Hartnett	1,867
Sandberg	1,752
B. Herman	1,710

AT-BATS

Banks	9,421
Anson	9,108
B. Williams	8,479
Santo	7,768
Hack	7,278
Ryan	6,770
Cavarretta	6,592
Kessinger	6,355
Hartnett	6,282
Sandberg	6,087

BATTING AVG

R. Stephenson	.336
Madlock	.336
Anson	.334
Lange	.330
Cuyler	.325
Everett	.323
H. Wilson	.322
M. Kelly	.316
Gore	.315
Ryan	.310

RUNS BATTED IN

Anson	1,715
Banks	1,636
B. Williams	1,354
Santo	1,290
Hartnett	1,153
Ryan	914
Cavarretta	896
Nicholson	833
H. Wilson	768
Sandberg	749

HOME RUNS

Banks	512
B. Williams	392
Santo	337
Hartnett	231
Sandberg	205
Nicholson	205
Sauer	198
H. Wilson	190
Dawson	152
Durham	138

DOUBLES

Anson	532
Banks	407
B. Williams	402
Hartnett	391
Hack	363
Ryan	362
Santo	353
B. Herman	346
Cavarretta	341
Sandberg	288

RUNS

Anson	1,719
Ryan	1,410
B. Williams	1,306
Banks	1,305
Hack	1,239
Santo	1,109
Sandberg	974
Cavarretta	968
Dahlen	918
B. Herman	875

STOLEN BASES

Chance	404
Tinker	304
Sandberg	297
Evers	291
Schulte	214
Slagle	198
Hack	165
Sheckard	163
Cuyler	161
Hofman	158

AUTOGRAPH PAGES

BIBLIOGRAPHY

Aylesworth, Thomas. *Baseball's Great Dynasties: The Cubs.* New York: Gallery Books, 1990.

Bosco, Joseph. *The Boys Who Would Be Cubs: A Year in the Heart of Baseball's Minor Leagues.* New York: William Morrow, 1990.

Falkner, David. *The Short Season: The Hard Work and High Times of Baseball in the Spring.* New York: Times Books, 1986.

Gold, Eddie, and Art Ahrens. *Cubs: The Renewal Era.* Chicago: Bonus Books, 1990.

Langford, Jim. *The Game Is Never Over: An Appreciative History of the Chicago Cubs, 1948–1980.* South Bend, Ind.: Icarus Press, 1982.

Ritter, Lawrence. *The Unforgettable Season.* New York: Holt, Rhinehart and Winston, 1981.

Seymour, Harold. *Baseball: The Early Years.* New York: Oxford University Press, 1960.

Shatzkin, Mike. *The Ballplayers.* New York: William Morrow, 1990.

Talley, Rick. *The Cubs of '69: Recollections of the Team That Should Have Been.* Chicago: Contemporary Books, 1989.

INDEX

PHOTOGRAPHY CREDITS

All photographs by David M. Spindel, with the following exceptions:

AP/Wide World Photos: pp. 73 top right, 76 top left, 79, 85 top, 99, 103, 123; Chicago Historical Society: p. 43; Chicago Sun Times: pp. 98, 101; National Baseball Library & Archive, Cooperstown, New York: pp. 18, 20, 21 bottom, 22, 24, 26, 32, 34, 41 top right, 45 bottom, 50, 52, 54, 55 top and bottom, 59 left, 67 bottom, 68, 70 top right and bottom, 71 top, 77, 85 bottom right, 94, 102 bottom left, 105 top, 106 bottom, 107 top, 108, 122 bottom, 127, 131; Photofile, Elmsford, New York: p. 120; UPI/Bettmann: pp. 2-3, 74 top, 84 bottom, 86 top, 88, 100

Take Me Out to the Ballgame, p. 13, by Jack Norworth and Albert Von Tilzer (1908)